in_focus

Fighting
Poverty
with Facts

in_**focus**

IDRC's *in_focus* Collection tackles current and pressing issues in sustainable international development. Each publication distills IDRC's research experience with an eye to drawing out important lessons, observations, and recommendations. Each also serves as a focal point for an IDRC website that probes more deeply into the issue, and is constructed to serve the differing information needs of IDRC's various readers. A full list of *in_focus* websites may be found at **www.idrc.ca/in_focus**. Each *in_focus* book may be browsed and ordered online at **www.idrc.ca/books**.

IDRC welcomes any feedback on this publication. Please direct your comments to The Publisher at **info@idrc.ca**.

in_**focus**

Fighting
Poverty
with Facts

COMMUNITY-BASED MONITORING SYSTEMS

Celia Reyes and Evan Due

INTERNATIONAL DEVELOPMENT RESEARCH CENTRE
Ottawa • Cairo • Dakar • Montevideo • Nairobi • New Delhi • Singapore

Published by the International Development Research Centre
PO Box 8500, Ottawa, ON, Canada K1G 3H9
www.idrc.ca / info@idrc.ca

Library and Archives Canada Cataloguing in Publication

Reyes, Celia
Fighting poverty with facts : community-based monitoring systems /
by Celia Reyes and Evan Due.

(In focus)
Available also on the Internet.
Includes bibliographical references: p.
ISBN 978-1-55250-432-1

1. Poverty—Research—Developing countries—Citizen participation.
2. Poverty—Research—Methodology.
3. Poor—Developing countries.
4. Community development—Developing countries.
I. Due, Evan
II. International Development Research Centre (Canada)
III. Title.
IV. Series: In focus (International Development Research Centre (Canada))

HC59.72 P6 R49 2009   362.5'525091724   C2009-980029-2
ISBN (ebook) 978-1-55250-435-2

This publication may be read online at **www.idrc.ca/books**, and serves as
the focal point for an IDRC thematic website on community-based poverty
monitoring systems: **www.idrc.ca/in_focus_poverty.**

Mixed Sources
Product group from well-managed
forests and other controlled sources
www.fsc.org Cert no. SGS-COC-3022
© 1996 Forest Stewardship Council

Contents

Executive Summary

The Issue

For more than two decades, governments and development agencies around the world have focused on reducing poverty. Although tremendous strides have been made, approximately one in four people in developing countries continues to live below the World Bank's international poverty line.

Wise public investment is key to reducing poverty and addressing inequalities within society. That requires timely and accurate data to measure progress and plan for investment, as well as for good analysis and policy application. In much of the developing world, however, the lack of appropriate local information about the poor hinders development planning and programs, and constrains efforts to monitor change. It also impedes efforts to measure progress toward achieving the Millennium Development Goals (MDGs).

For more than a decade, IDRC has supported researchers in 15 countries of Asia and Africa who have developed, tested, and implemented a community-based poverty monitoring system (CBMS). This book, and its accompanying website and enclosed CD, argue that good public policy choices for empowering and uplifting the poor are best made when local authorities and communities work together and are guided by sound data and evidence-based analysis. This is key to ensuring effective public spending and greater public accountability.

The Research

The research has shown that CBMS is not a turnkey solution. It requires adaptation to specific on-the-ground conditions and the political, economic, and social environment. And as the various country experiences show, real benefits quickly accrue to communities as well as to their governments, from new crucial services such as schools and sanitation facilities to health and employment programs. CBMS gives communities a voice in decision-making.

The Philippines: From cradle to national implementation

Beginning in the province of Palawan, CBMS has spread to 52 of the country's 81 provinces. The goal: 100% coverage by 2010. Local governments use CBMS data to prepare annual investment plans and to prioritize projects for poverty reduction, to evaluate the impacts of their projects, and to prepare for emergencies. And the researchers note, CBMS has also increased local governments' transparency and accountability.

Vietnam: Focusing on basic needs in communes

"Because of this census, we have information we have never had before," says a commune chairman in the very poor Nho Quan district. "Based on this data we can make plans." Among those plans and programs has been vocational training in such areas as traditional crafts to generate employment, assistance to improve inadequate housing, and the provision of agricultural inputs to boost food production. The data is also helping Vietnam monitor progress toward the MDGs.

Cambodia: Improving local statistics and governance

When the CBMS survey in Kbal Snoul village showed how many children did not attend school because none was accessible, a donor stepped forward to build a new school within walking distance. CBMS results have helped poor Cambodian communities attract donor assistance. They have also enabled communities to better deal with their own problems, including domestic violence.

Burkina Faso: Empowering the poor

Because of the high level of illiteracy, communicating the CBMS results back to the community posed a particular challenge in Burkina Faso. The solution: translate the data into easy-to-interpret drawings posted at village assembly offices and into the local languages.

Senegal: Supporting the PRSP

Developed to support the Poverty Reduction Strategy Paper (PRSP) process, the Senegal CBMS demonstrates the importance of community validation of data.

For more case studies and further details on those presented above, visit **www.idrc.ca/in_focus_poverty**.

The Lessons

Regardless of where it has been carried out, CBMS has permitted the acquisition of a richer body of information and data on the welfare of the poor. It has also enabled poor local communities to assert their needs to their local and national governments and influence budgetary allocations. As such, CBMS has become a direct instrument for empowerment and actual poverty reduction.

Lessons learned about the enabling conditions

➤ Decentralization facilitates the adoption of CBMS.

➤ Political commitment is key to sustainability.

➤ Public participation is important.

➤ CBMS is cost-effective.

Lessons learned about CBMS design and implementation

➤ Partnerships between researchers, government officials, and communities are essential.

- Enlisting and orienting the community determines success from the outset.

- Selecting indicators and developing survey tools require research.

- Adequate training should not be underestimated.

- Data collection and processing must be done in a timely manner.

- Validating the data is essential.

- Dissemination is crucial.

Lessons learned about the benefits of CBMS

- CBMS empowers the community by building its capacity to participate in diagnosing the problem and offering solutions.

- CBMS improves the allocation of resources by making it easier to prioritize interventions.

- CBMS increases equity in resource allocation.

- CBMS helps to monitor the impact of projects and programs, thus contributing to poverty-reduction efforts.

Foreword

The passage of the Local Government Code in 1991 has put the spotlight on Local Government Units (LGUs), particularly on the huge responsibility that was entrusted to them as well as the amount of resources that are now at their disposal to effectively discharge the devolved functions. In the report of the Union of Local Authorities of the Philippines, they noted the increasing share of local governments in national internal revenues. For the period 1991–2001, the average Internal Revenue Allotment per year was PHP79.96 billion,[1] or 13.83% of the national budget.

The vast amount of resources that is now under their control dramatically highlights the importance of making sure that they are equipped with the right tools, systems, and procedures to ensure an effective use of public financial resources. One way of

---

[1]As of 31 March 2009, 48.25 Philippine pesos (PHP) = US$1.

doing this is by providing them with access to comprehensive socioeconomic data, such as the data generated by the Community-Based Monitoring System or CBMS, on the basis of which they can craft their development plans.

This is especially evident in the Philippines, the birthplace of CBMS, where CBMS data is now being used for facilitating evidence-based planning and budgeting in 13 498 *barangays* in 531 municipalities, 42 cities and 52 provinces. Since it was pilot-tested in the 1990s, the CBMS has been transplanted to 14 other countries in Asia and Africa. Indeed, the exuberance with which these LGUs have embraced CBMS can only be a glowing testament to how it has effectively responded to a long-felt need for a system that can provide a reliable and credible information base at the local level for policymaking, program design, and impact monitoring.

The Philippine Government has been very supportive of this initiative. For instance, the Medium-Term Philippine Development Plan 2004–2010 targets the expansion of CBMS coverage to all LGUs by 2010. Several memorandum circulars and policy issuances have likewise been prepared by key national government agencies supporting the use of CBMS as a monitoring tool to diagnose poverty at the local level as well as to localize the Millennium Development Goals (MDGs):

➤ The NEDA (National Economic and Development Authority) Board Social Development Committee issued Resolution No. 3 series of 2006 enjoining all national government agencies and LGUs to adopt the CBMS as the systematic monitoring tool to diagnose the poverty situation at the local level.

➤ The National Anti-Poverty Commission has issued an En Banc Resolution No. 7 (issued in March 2003) directing LGUs to adopt the 13 core local poverty indicators as the minimum set of community-based information for poverty diagnosis and planning at the local level.

➤ The Department of the Interior and Local Government has issued Memorandum Circulars 2003-92 (April 2003) to set policy guidelines for the adoption of the 13 core local poverty indicators for planning and 2004-152 (November 2004) to encourage LGUs to intensify efforts toward the achievement of the MDGs. The latter cicular also enjoins LGUs to use monitoring systems such as MBN-CBIS, CBMS, IRAP, etc., in monitoring the nature and extent of poverty.

➤ The National Statistical Coordination Board (NSCB) has also issued Resolution No. 6 (2005) which recognizes and enjoins support to the CBMS as a tool for strengthening the statistical system at the local level. It also directs NSCB Technical Staff to initiate and coordinate an advocacy program for the adoption of CBMS by the LGUs, through the Regional Statistical Coordinating Committee, the technical arm of the NSCB Executive Board in the regions.

➤ The League of Municipalities of the Philippines has also issued Memorandum Circulars 027-2006 and 027-2006B enjoining member LGUs to adopt (or sustain the adoption of) the CBMS as a tool for local poverty diagnosis and to institutionalize this as part of the system of local governance. At the same time, the League has issued these circulars to ensure the incorporation of the MDG targets and utilization of the CBMS data in the local development plans at the municipal and *barangay* levels for focused poverty targeting.

We believe that CBMS represents a significant step forward in the nation's struggle to allow more Filipino families a just share of the national wealth and, as such, deserves the support and commitment of all who believe that a brighter, more prosperous future awaits our nation and people in the years ahead.

Domingo F. Panganiban
Secretary & Lead Coordinator
National Anti-Poverty Commission
Philippines

Preface

Primary schools for children where none existed before in remote areas of Cambodia, vocational training programs for poor rural women in Vietnam, daycare centres and sanitation facilities in the Philippines — these are just a few of the services provided by local governments after a participatory poverty monitoring system clearly identified communities' most pressing needs. The data provided by the surveys has also enabled local governments to obtain resources from donors for development projects. It has helped governments identify priority actions to help reduce poverty among their populations. In Laos and elsewhere, it has helped pinpoint who should be targeted for assistance. And it has mobilized communities to take action to address some of their problems themselves — primary school enrolment doubled in one Burkina Faso village, for instance, without additional schools being built, and villagers set up communal vegetable gardens to reduce hunger, a key indicator of poverty.

These are just a few examples of what can be achieved when communities and governments have current, accurate data on which to base their planning — data provided by implementing the Community-Based Monitoring System (CBMS) described in this book. IDRC has been supporting CBMS since its inception under the Micro Impacts of Macroeconomic and Adjustment Policies (MIMAP) program in the early 1990s and has been actively involved throughout its development and expansion in the Philippines, as well as to many other countries in Asia and Africa.

CBMS started as a monitoring system in the early 1990s to provide information on the impact of macroeconomic policies and structural adjustment programs on households and individuals. It was expected that these policies and programs would affect households differently and that safety nets need to be put in place to assist these vulnerable groups. But the data coming from national statistical offices was not disaggregated enough to be able to capture this. A local monitoring system that could complement the national system was therefore needed. Moreover, as countries have moved to decentralize as a means of bringing governments closer to the people, the demand for local information has increased.

Unfortunately, this shift to a decentralized government structure has not been accompanied by a corresponding shift in the statistical system. The statistical systems in many developing countries have remained focused on meeting the information needs of central governments. Thus, CBMS has been designed to provide information that would be useful primarily to local governments, and secondarily to national governments and other stakeholders. It is intended to improve local governance and promote transparency and accountability by providing information that can facilitate evidence-based decision making.

The CBMS strategy of involving local communities in research and knowledge sharing, building capacity among local researchers and the users of research, and generating evidence-based information essential for planning and policy-making reflects IDRC's fundamental approach to development research. IDRC strongly believes in involving local communities as partners in research and in listening to the poor, who know better than anyone else what their poverty condition is and how to improve their lives. CBMS empowers them by ensuring their participation in the development process and by generating knowledge for appropriate policy responses.

The CBMS work has been premised on the fact that, to be effective, development programs must be targeted and based on relevant, current, accurate, disaggregated data. CBMS addresses information gaps in development planning by institutionalizing systematic data collection and validation at the local level for use by local authorities. Technical collaboration between the CBMS Network team at the Angelo King Institute of De La Salle University, led by Celia Reyes, and partner local governments has ensured that the information collected accurately reflects realities on the ground and can be readily used in policy and planning. It is therefore not surprising that CBMS has developed into an indispensable tool for local government planners and policymakers. How this has been done in different countries is described in this book.

International commitments to meeting the Millennium Development Goals (MDGs) has made it imperative that countries collect reliable and timely information to monitor progress and develop comprehensive strategies and programs to meet these goals. CBMS allows this to be realized by localizing the MDGs and providing the tools and policy space for real development to take place.

This book is about how CBMS has been developed, adapted, and implemented in various corners of the globe and how the evidence it yields has and can be used to reduce poverty. Because CBMS is first and foremost a participatory survey methodology that must be applied rigorously, we focus on technical aspects of development and implementation. Descriptions of how the system has been adapted in different countries point to its flexibility and to the various purposes it can and does serve.

This book shows how a local monitoring system can be designed and implemented to respond to local needs and capabilities in different developing countries, and how analysis of data generated from CBMS can be used by local and national policymakers to help reduce poverty. It also shows how local decision-making can benefit from the use of locally generated data and processes. This book is about local government officials who are committed to helping the poor move out of poverty, and about communities who have been empowered by the data and the space to participate in the crafting of local plans and budgets.

Of all those involved in the preparation of this book, we owe our greatest thanks to IDRC's chief writer, Michelle Hibler. This book would not have been possible without her constant help, encouragement, and expertise. We also thank Bill Carman and Rowena Beamish, of IDRC's Communications Division, for their careful editing work. This book has greatly benefited from the comments and suggestions provided by colleagues within IDRC, the Poverty and Economic Policy (PEP) network, as well as a number of external reviewers. Our thanks to all of them. We also extend our gratitude to the CBMS project team leaders who responded to our requests for information. Likewise, we wish to recognize and acknowledge the Philippine CBMS team for their unwavering commitment to building the capacity of local governments so that the poor will be served.

Celia Reyes is Senior Research Fellow at the Philippine Institute for Development Studies and leader of the Community-Based Monitoring System subnetwork of the global Policy and Economic Policy research network. Dr Reyes obtained her doctorate in economics from the University of Pennsylvania. Her areas of research include poverty monitoring systems, poverty analysis, and macro-econometric modeling.

Evan Due is Senior Program Specialist responsible for economics and trade programs at IDRC's Singapore office. His research interests include public policy, institutional economics, and poverty analysis. Before joining IDRC, he served in various positions with the Canadian International Development Agency, including diplomatic assignments in Pakistan, Afghanistan, and India, and headed Canada's delegation to the OECD Development Assistance Committee's working parties on the financial aspects of poverty reduction.

12 January 2009

Part 1

The Issue and Development Context

"The availability of good statistics and the capacity of governments, donors and international organizations to systematically measure, monitor and report on progress in all social and economic spheres are at the heart of development policy and the achievement of the MDGs."

— *The Millennium Development Goals Report 2007* (UN 2007, p. 34)

For more than two decades, governments and development agencies around the world have focused on reducing poverty. Although tremendous strides have been made, approximately one in four people in developing countries continues to live below the World Bank's international poverty line of US$1.25 per day (Chen and Ravallion 2008). Progress has also been markedly uneven, ranging from the dramatic success experienced in East Asia (notably China), to relatively slower progress in South Asia and Latin America, to deeper poverty in sub-Saharan Africa.

Material deprivation based on income and consumption measures forms only part of the picture. Understanding and measuring the well-being of the poor also requires a more multi-faceted approach that takes into account other kinds of deprivation, such as health, education, access to public goods and services, security, freedom, and human rights. While national and global accounts are critical benchmarks, poverty and inequality are more accurately measured and understood within the specific geographical, economic, social, and political contexts in which people live, at household and community levels.

Wise public investment is key to reducing poverty and addressing inequalities within society. Timely and accurate data is required to measure progress and plan for that investment. It is also essential for good analysis and policy application. As *The Millennium Development Goals Report 2007* states, "Sound national statistical systems and enhanced public accountability are necessary to support all these efforts" (UN 2007). And as Christopher Scott of the London School of Economics notes, "Strengthening the evidence base of policy-making in developing countries has always been important, but it has become particularly crucial in the current period.... No less than 55 countries lack information on the share of the population living in poverty [and] nearly double that number have no data on poverty trends, so that progress towards the MDGs cannot be tracked directly over time" (Scott 2005).

In much of the developing world, the lack of appropriate local information about the poor hinders development planning and programs, and constrains efforts to monitor change. This book presents one system, developed with IDRC support, that can help governments formulate more effective poverty programs and monitor their impact, as well as measure progress toward the Millennium Development Goals (MDGs). Known as the Community-Based Monitoring System (CBMS), this system shows that a meaningful approach to understanding and tackling poverty requires involving local communities in public policy decisions.

As we explain, good public policy choices for empowering and uplifting the poor are best made when local authorities and communities work together and are guided by sound data and evidence-based analysis. This, we argue, is key to ensuring effective public spending and greater public accountability.

The research presented in this book stresses that the poor must be involved in planning public programs that affect their livelihoods and well-being. Policy decisions must respond to their concerns, build on their knowledge and experience, and consider them as participants in the policy process. Engaging communities to work with local authorities to monitor and use locally obtained, verifiable information about actual living conditions for planning purposes is what many CBMS practitioners refer to as "localizing the MDGs."

Measuring and monitoring poverty

Throughout the 1990s, the international development community was galvanized to improve perspectives on poverty by better understanding the multi-dimensional nature of poverty, as well as its distribution and depth. In part, this was driven by research from international agencies showing that the poor and vulnerable were adversely affected by external shocks and macroeconomic adjustment and needed special attention when formulating public policies (see, for example, Jolly 1991). The World Bank's 1990 *World Development Report: Poverty (WDR)* was particularly instrumental in focusing international attention on poverty in developing countries and on strategies for targeting the poor. It highlighted dimensions of poverty other than income, the characteristics of the poor — who they are, where they live, and what factors contribute to their poverty (such as lack of assets, education, and health) — as well as issues of inequality. The report also generated attention around measuring poverty through improved statistical surveys and poverty estimations.

However, for the most part, monetary measures for assessing poverty remained dominant and shaped poverty-reduction approaches, even those promoted through more "Comprehensive Development Frameworks" and the "Poverty Reduction Strategy Papers" (PRSPs) process that largely replaced the structural adjustment programs of the World Bank. Less progress was made in evolving strategies and policies that responded significantly to the underlying processes by which the poor remained in poverty, or moved out of it.

While governments continued to emphasize top-down approaches to address poverty and largely income- and consumption-driven national poverty-reduction programs, there was growing recognition of the importance of targeting the poor and of the need to better understand the "micro" aspects and "dynamics" of poverty.

A decade after the 1990 *WDR*, the World Bank revisited the progress made toward reducing poverty and advocated a more comprehensive, inclusive, and pro-poor driven approach. The *WDR 2000/2001: Attacking Poverty*, led by economist Ravi Kanbur, was a much more comprehensive analysis of poverty and marked an important departure: it broadened the concept of poverty to include vulnerability, the dynamics of powerlessness, and risk — what Amartya Sen referred to as "the capabilities that a person has...to lead the kind of life he or she values" (Sen 1999).

The inclusion of participatory and combined methods of poverty monitoring, such as household surveys and capability measures, were introduced to provide a more accurate and "experiential" view of poverty as felt and expressed by the poor themselves. Measures of factors such as powerlessness, security, and other participatory dimensions highlighted the importance of "governance and accountability" in the poverty debate. It also emphasized the importance of context in understanding poverty, the views of those who are experiencing poverty, and the means and policies needed to address it.

The importance of measuring and monitoring the multi-dimensional aspects of poverty — and of measurements for assessing progress toward the MDGs — is now widely accepted. However, there is conspicuously less consensus on the empirical applications of methodologies, or agreement on how to translate this into operational policies. As the *WDR 2000/2001* points out, "Developing countries need to prepare their own mix of policies to reduce poverty, reflecting national priorities and local realities. Choices will depend on the economic, sociopolitical, structural, and cultural context of individual countries — indeed, individual communities." But, paradoxically, the World Bank and the international donor community have continued to lead in developing poverty frameworks in most recipient countries, largely without locally driven research perspectives.

It is in this context of trying to understand and apply local perspectives of poverty to development strategies that CBMS evolved. Its origins and development as an approach to bridging methods of poverty measurement with strategies for evidence-based planning, accountable public investment, and community empowerment, are explained in Part 2. The development of CBMS is not linear, however, nor is it a blueprint. As the country experiences described in Part 3 show, CBMS works best where institutional and political factors at the local community level are supportive.

Generating information for accountability

Poverty-reduction strategies require measuring and continually monitoring the dynamics of well-being. Involving the poor in this process is vital. The institutional and social context by which the poor can express their voice through their communities and have their information meaningfully communicated for better public service delivery is fundamental. This ensures that public resources are effectively used and that accountability and local governance are strengthened.

Governments are responsible for providing public goods and services that can reduce poverty. However, as research has shown throughout the developing world, the allocation of public resources for development does not itself ensure that services are provided, efficiently or at all, or are accessible to the poor. The poor, the providers, and the policymakers need to be effectively linked and the relationships between them mediated by institutions that favour inclusiveness and a framework of accountability.

Decentralization and subsidiarity — the principle that states that matters should be handled by the smallest (or the lowest) competent authority — often facilitate such a framework because they empower the poor by providing them with better information. According to the World Bank, this transfer of political, fiscal, and administrative functions from national to sub-national governments has emerged as one of the most important trends in development policy. Decentralization has also been widely supported by donors as a means to broaden public participation and local ownership of development programs (Jütting et al. 2004).

While an important enabling condition, decentralization of public functions in and of itself does not assure the necessary conditions for poverty reduction, especially where institutional and legal frameworks are weak, political will is lacking, and there is little public accountability. Research has shown that decentralization has led to different poverty outcomes, depending on how well local governments have been able to execute federal functions, the commitment to reforms, and how social institutions and political structures have supported local participation in development programs. Critical to this process is the role of information in raising citizens' awareness of how public resources are allocated, by whom, and under what conditions.

The Philippines is one country where decentralization has had a significantly positive impact on service delivery and poverty reduction. Other Asian countries, such as Indonesia, Vietnam, and Cambodia, are also moving down this path. Yet, where institutional or political factors are not supportive, where there is less transparency around public expenditures, or where capacity does not exist to implement policies, decentralization may not have the desired outcomes (Jütting et al. 2004).

Many countries in Africa, as we discuss in Part 3, are still at early stages of decentralization. The key challenges they face include the clear assignment of functions; the development of effective fiscal transfer mechanisms; the accountability of local governments; and the capacity of local governments to effectively plan, manage, and monitor public resources.

Experience has shown that, over the long run, CBMS is most effective where the provision of public goods is decentralized to local governments and where local communities participate in the policy-making process by providing information about their needs and aspirations. This linkage also helps to generate important feedback on the impacts of policy interventions, enabling policymakers to make more informed decisions in the future.

Local ownership of development

Despite the push for a "pro-poor, local development-driven" agenda, few developing countries have actually been in the driver's seat of the poverty-reduction effort. And this has been acutely reflected in the lack of capacity in local institutions. As IDRC Vice-President Rohinton Medora has noted, "Little was done to build indigenous capacity for research and policy analysis," a crucial element to sustain efforts to measure and analyze poverty.

The promise that poverty assessment and poverty-reduction programs will become locally owned has long been a guiding principle of the OECD Development Assistance Committee of donors. Yet, despite the rhetoric, the PRSPs, and the glossy reports from international development agencies, the process of development planning remains largely asymmetric in favour of donor approaches. Only recently have there emerged poverty-reduction agendas based on locally conducted research and capacity-building activities that are nationally based and funded. These are particularly evident in emerging economies such as Thailand. Fundamental to this transition has been the generation of local knowledge within institutes of higher learning and research organizations.

There are no shortcuts to building local capacity. However, some paths are being firmly laid and followed by others in the developing regions of the world. This book shows how one local network of developing-country researchers was created out of a need to counteract this asymmetry and to establish ownership over local information and knowledge. It also describes how this eventually transformed into a dynamic relationship involving local governments and local communities for meaningful development planning. This is about the experience of the CBMS network of researchers in systematically collecting and analyzing locally generated information to better understand the impacts of public policies and programs on the poor.

According to Christopher Scott, establishing an effective institutional framework to deliver evidence-based policy-making is a long, slow process for most countries. CBMS can help reduce that time and fill in gaps. As explained in Part 2 and illustrated in Part 3, CBMS is a system that effectively increases the capacity of local government administrations to plan and budget, to monitor programs and projects, and to report on MDG targets with a high degree of reliability and precision. It also enables local government agencies to design targeted poverty alleviation programs and other public interventions that are responsive to, and can be tracked by, communities. In doing so, it empowers the poor.

Part 2

The Approach

"The efforts to measure, monitor and report on progress towards the MDGs have highlighted the need to improve most developing countries' capacity to produce, analyse and disseminate data."

— *The Millennium Development Goals Report 2008* (UN 2008, p. 50)

On the web

THE RESEARCH

As explained in Part 1, knowing who the poor are, where they are, and why they are poor is essential for addressing poverty. But despite efforts to measure, describe, and analyze poverty, understanding it through the eyes of the poor continues to elude many policymakers and planners.

Recognizing the importance of understanding poverty from the perspective of the poor themselves and conveying this information to policymakers, the Community-Based Monitoring System (CBMS) was developed in the Philippines in the 1990s. It emerged in response to the need for a poverty-monitoring system that was adapted to local contexts and capacities, conducted by local researchers, and intended for local-level planners.

The system needed to capture the various dimensions of poverty in an ongoing, dynamic way, and to allow the poor themselves to validate the information in collaboration with local officials and planners. Why? Because this makes it easier to diagnose the extent and nature of poverty, to formulate appropriate responses, to allocate resources to identified beneficiaries, and to assess the impact of policies and programs. In doing so, CBMS aims to reduce poverty.

CBMS initially evolved as a specific research project funded by IDRC. But as the activities described later in this book show, it has taken on an instrumental and independent role to provide local government officials and policymakers with a regular source of information on core development indicators at the household level. Because nationally aggregated data from surveys and censuses cannot provide detailed, current, local information useful for local government, the demand for CBMS-generated data has grown, especially where government functions are decentralized. As an easy-to-use and cost-effective tool for local government planning agencies, it is now being adopted, supported, and institutionalized within local governments throughout the Philippines as well as in other countries in Asia and Africa.

The origins of CBMS

The need for a multi-dimensional approach to poverty referred to in the previous chapter played an important role in the development of participatory monitoring and evaluation (PME) activities worldwide. In the Philippines and elsewhere, these initiatives promoted the participation of communities — initially in areas of natural resource management — as beneficiaries in monitoring development project outputs. Development agencies promoted these programs as part of their development projects to track their progress and account to donors. Because they were linked intrinsically to specific development projects, PME activities tended to remain tied to the largely externally financed programs and usually only spanned the life of the projects themselves. Consequently, they were not institutionalized into more sustainable local systems within government.

CBMS did not originate as a PME activity. Instead, it developed organically out of an indigenous research initiative, in response to local researchers' interest in monitoring the impacts of macro-adjustment policies on local communities and households. This initiative began as a series of locally led inquiries on how macro-economic adjustment policies affected households and firms. The initial research pointed out that macro reforms can have negative and unintended consequences, and that policymakers can introduce inappropriate policies because they lack good field studies of how households — especially the poor — behave and are affected. This laid the foundations for an IDRC program called Micro Impacts of Macroeconomic and Adjustment Policies, or MIMAP.

The MIMAP program

Micro Impacts of Macroeconomic and Adjustment Policies

In any country, access to adequate information is key to designing economic policies that will have a favourable impact on the poor and vulnerable. Unless governments understand the dynamics of poverty, the less fortunate are likely to lose out when new economic policies are implemented.

In 1989, IDRC created the Micro Impacts of Macroeconomic and Adjustment Policies (MIMAP) program to help developing countries find alternatives to traditional macroeconomic policies by meshing policy analysis with poverty monitoring. The goal was to help these countries minimize the negative impact of structural adjustment programs on the poor. MIMAP's aim was to increase the understanding of poverty and promote dialogue among researchers, politicians, government officials, and non-governmental organizations (NGOs) so that more equitable policies could be developed.

From an initial project in the Philippines, the network grew to include more than 40 research teams from Asia, Africa, and Canada. The work is continuing through the Poverty and Economic Policy research network (www.pep-net.org), launched in 2002.

The research program emphasized the critical need for poverty measurement, monitoring, and analysis to be done at the local level, conducted by local researchers, and involving local stakeholders and policymakers. This gave rise to the establishment of a local network of Filipino researchers led by Celia Reyes, which came to be known as the CBMS Research Network.

In their assessment of existing systems, the CBMS research team found that various sets of data existed at the village, municipal, and provincial levels. But national sample surveys were not sufficiently disaggregated to track households over time. Moreover, the data was not returned to the communities. This meant that the communities could not compare how they were faring relative to others, nor could local leaders use the information for planning a wide range of public services, including targeted anti-poverty programs for which they were responsible. Other surveys, carried out by NGOs, were not comparable and were carried out at irregular intervals.

Basically, the lack of appropriate information at the local level constrained local governments from carrying out their decentralized functions and made them less accountable. It also reduced the effectiveness of public investment in fostering development and reducing poverty in communities.

The CBMS research team in the Philippines was convinced that the best way to address these data gaps was for local governments to work in partnership with residents — at the *barangay* or village level — in monitoring poverty and development. The CBMS researchers proposed such a system, to be piloted in sentinel sites. The team designed a simple Household Profile Questionnaire that used minimum basic needs indicators already present in many of the existing survey forms, but also included other key poverty indicators. The indicator list was purposely simple so that the survey could be easily administered and understood by local officials and community members. To the extent possible, it was also consistent with standard concepts and definitions used by national statistical offices.

The system was developed in consultation with local government officials, community representatives, and other stakeholders, according to the specific features of the locality in which it would be administered. Beginning in the two Philippine *barangays* of Masuso and Real de Cacarong in the province of Bulacan, the team was able to demonstrate the value of the system for local poverty monitoring and local-level planning to both local government officials and community representatives. And, as important, the process of data collection was found to build capacity and empower local communities as they became aware of their economic and social conditions. The pilot also enabled the team to evaluate the indicators and validate the information collected and processed by other agencies.

The pilot demonstrated that the CBMS was feasible. The survey generated most of the data needed by local governments and could be used to prepare their local development plans. The research also showed the areas in which local governments needed to increase their capabilities so that they could design and implement programs to address the needs of specific groups. The pilot further pointed to the need for training in survey enumeration, data processing and analysis, database maintenance, project identification, prioritization, monitoring, and budgeting (Reyes and Ilarde 1996).

The work of the CBMS team gained considerable popularity in the Philippines, leading to its initial uptake in 1999 when then-Governor of the province of Palawan, Salvador Socrates, invited the CBMS team to introduce the system province-wide. With the support of the provincial executive and line departments, CBMS demonstrated its sustainability as a local system adapted to local conditions.

What is CBMS?

What is CBMS and how does it differ from other poverty-monitoring instruments? CBMS is an organized way of collecting ongoing or recurring information at the local level to be used by local governments, national government agencies, NGOs, and civil society for planning, budgeting, and implementing local development programs, as well as for monitoring and evaluating their performance. Fundamentally, it is a tool for improved local governance and democratic decision-making that promotes greater transparency and accountability in resource allocation.

CBMS' five objectives are to

➤ diagnose the extent of poverty at the local level;

➤ formulate appropriate plans and programs to address problems;

➤ provide the basis for rational allocation of resources;

➤ identify eligible beneficiaries for targeted programs; and

➤ monitor and assess the impact of programs and projects.

What sets CBMS apart from other monitoring systems is that it is based on a partnership between local communities, local governments, and trained local researchers in an institutionalized system of regular data collection, validation, and analysis for local program development. Furthermore — and significantly — it builds the capacity of local governments to use poverty statistics in formulating development plans and poverty-reduction programs. It also builds the capacity of the local communities through information. "CBMS implementation is itself a poverty-reduction policy," says Louis-Marie Asselin of the Centre d'étude et de coopération internationale (CECI) and a MIMAP/CBMS trainer, "since one of its goals is the empowerment of local communities."

CBMS is grounded in the principle that poverty can best be understood through the lives and experiences of the poor themselves. It tracks poverty and development at the household level at regular intervals through a set of basic indicators (Table 1). The data is collected and analyzed by trained community members, in partnership with local government officials, for use by local development planners. The method can be applied quickly, inexpensively, and frequently. It is easy to sustain and is easily conducted by trained local fieldworkers. The principal aim is to reduce poverty, but there are other important associated benefits, such as increased capacity of local government officials and community representatives in development planning, increased gender equity, environmental sensitization, and even early warning of crisis impacts.

CBMS has a number of distinctive features:

➤ it is a census of households and not a sample survey.

➤ it is rooted in local government and promotes community participation.

➤ it uses local personnel and community volunteers as monitors.

➤ it has a core set of simple, well-established indicators.

➤ it establishes a databank at all geopolitical levels.

Moreover, the data can be disaggregated by region, gender, socio-economic group, age, ethnicity, and other variables. Because the monitoring exercises are conducted regularly and the results processed rapidly, the data is very useful for ongoing local-level planning. And because the results are accessible to anyone who wishes to see them, there is greater buy-in on the part of all stakeholders.

Table 1. Indicators at the core of CBMS

CBMS indicator	Dimensions of poverty	Core indicators
Survival	Health	Proportion of child deaths (0–5 years old)
		Proportion of women who died due to pregnancy-related causes
	Nutrition	Proportion of malnourished children (0–5 years old)
	Water and sanitation	Proportion of households without access to safe water supply
		Proportion of households without access to sanitary toilet facilities
Security	Shelter	Proportion of households living in makeshift housing
		Proportion of households classified as squatters/informal settlers
	Peace and order	Proportion of persons who were victims of crime
Enabling	Income	Proportion of households with income below the poverty threshold
		Proportion of households with income below the subsistence threshold
		Proportion of households that experienced food shortages
	Employment	Proportion of persons who are unemployed
	Education	Proportion of children 6–12 years old who are not in elementary school
		Proportion of children 13–16 who are not in secondary school

A household census

CBMS is unusual as a poverty-monitoring system in that it collects information on all households in the community. This is essential for informing special targeted poverty interventions such as cash transfers, health benefits, and other public sector entitlements.

Roots in the community

CBMS is locally owned by the communities and local governments, which take the lead in data collection and processing. They also keep the database and use the data to formulate annual development and investment plans. The data collected provides vital baseline information for preparing socio-economic profiles, project proposals, and other related development reports. CBMS data also serves as a barometer for gauging the effectiveness of programs and projects.

Making data available

Building a statistical database, kept in the community or local government, is an essential element of CBMS. To ensure that data is widely available to researchers, policy analysts, policymakers, and program implementers, the CBMS Network team is developing a central repository of CBMS data from all countries implementing the system through the Poverty and Economic Policy research network, launched in 2002.

Country	Year	Source of data	Number of households
Bangladesh	2004	6 wards in West-Muhammadpur Union	3 761
Benin	2005	13th District of Cotonou (6 city sectors)	12 337
	2006	District of Adogbe (3 villages)	823
	2006	District of Mededjonou (9 villages)	3 026
Cambodia	2006	181 villages in 3 provinces	22 298
Ghana	2004	3 communities in Dangme West District	5 379
Indonesia	2005	Cianjur and Demak Districts	5 379
Lao PDR	2004	4 villages in Sepone and Toomlan districts	458
Philippines	2000/07	15 provinces and 5 cities	1 145 142
Tanzania	2006	Kndege ward and Nala village	4 901
Vietnam	2006	42 communes in 5 provinces	42 000

Community engagement

Community participation is critical to the success of CBMS. Informed from the outset about the survey's objectives and uses, the community provides enumerators to collect the data, as well as personnel to process and analyze it. Information is collected from every household and the data is tallied and consolidated at the village level. The processed data is returned to the community for validation and discussion. This empowers communities by providing them with information and a process through which they can actively participate in diagnosing poverty and identifying appropriate interventions, including allocating resources. Because community members are involved in data collection and validation, CBMS develops the capability of communities to generate and use data. It facilitates the dissemination of data collected to the next higher geopolitical level for immediate action and, ultimately, reaches national planners. The system also uses the information generated by existing monitoring systems as supplemental information.

A core set of indicators

A requisite for establishing a good poverty monitoring system is first determining what to monitor. The CBMS core indicators capture multiple dimensions of poverty. Easy to collect and process, the system is flexible and accommodates community-specific indicators. For instance, the Philippine province of Camarines Norte includes indicators related to natural calamities. In Ninh Binh province, Vietnam, indicators have been added to determine women's well-being. In Tanzania, child labour is measured. In Ghana, an indicator covers access to community services such as banks and the post office. And because the CBMS indicators are sensitive to gender differences, the data can also show how girls and boys, and men and women are affected differently by policies and benefit unequally from programs. For example, a survey in one Vietnamese commune showed local officials that many children had dropped out of school because their families could no longer afford to send them. Boys and girls were affected equally, but not for the same reasons: the boys quit because of travel costs; the girls, to work in the fields.

Together, the indicators provide information not only on how poor a community is, but also on who in the community is poor, and where. Figure 1 shows how information from CBMS can complement national surveys.

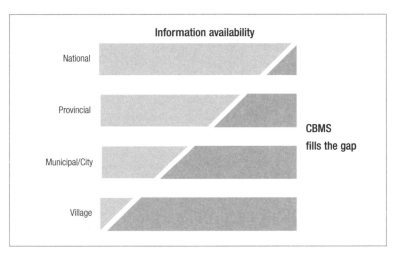

Figure 1. Complementing national surveys with CBMS.

CBMS step by step

"CBMS consists of doing very simple things," says CECI's Louis-Marie Asselin. But once the data is generated, you can do very sophisticated things with it, as with survey data from national statistical offices. "It is worthwhile to do this simple thing," he adds, "but it must be done correctly." Implementing a community-based monitoring system requires following a number of steps.

Advocacy and organization

Data requirements and existing monitoring systems must be evaluated to identify gaps and develop a work plan that details the commitment of all parties and the involvement of key human resources at all levels, as well as the financial and physical resources for training, data collection, processing, validation, database management, and dissemination. The commitment of the local government to use the data must be ensured.

Collecting and editing data

Questionnaires are developed for household and community surveys, enumerators are identified and trained, and the community is informed. The data is collected through a household survey and/or focus group discussions. Local personnel are identified and trained as enumerators and field supervisors.

Encoding data

The data gathered is tallied and consolidated by community members trained to do this work. The encoding system can be manual or computerized, depending on resources and capabilities. Computerized encoding facilitates data analysis and mapping.

Processing data

Processing is a critical step since the results form the basis for local planning and program implementation. Wherever possible, computerized processing is initiated, even at the village level. Village-level aggregates are then submitted to higher geopolitical levels for consolidation.

Validation and consultation

The results of the census are presented in a community forum where the extent of poverty in its different dimensions is assessed and discussed, the causes of poverty are diagnosed and explained, and priority needs and appropriate interventions are identified.

CBMS — An eight-step process
Step 1 – Advocacy/organization
Step 2 – Data collection and field editing
Step 3 – Data encoding and map digitization
Step 4 – Processing and mapping
Step 5 – Data validation and community consultation
Step 6 – Knowledge (database) management
Step 7 – Plan formulation
Step 8 – Dissemination, implementation, and monitoring

Presenting the processed data to the community is vital to CBMS implementation, both to ensure data accuracy and obtain explanations for the findings.

Establishing a database
Databanks are established at each geopolitical level for planning and monitoring purposes. This ensures access to census results by various stakeholders.

Formulating plans
The CBMS data and its analysis serve as inputs in preparing annual development plans and socio-economic profiles at all levels of government. They also provide benchmark information for enriching the resource profiles of project sites of NGOs and other donors. Data from the CBMS also helps to identify eligible beneficiaries for poverty-reduction programs.

Disseminating findings
CBMS results are made available to planning bodies, program implementers, and other interested groups through data boards, computerized databanks, publications, workshops, and forums, among other means, including on the Internet.

On the web

THE RESEARCH

Resources needed

CBMS requires resources — human, financial, and physical. It is, however, an extremely cost-effective tool for local governments. Partnerships ensure resource availability and success. To implement the system, key government personnel from community to provincial levels participate as monitors, field supervisors, survey enumerators, and data processors.

Local governments generally cover the various recurrent costs in implementing CBMS. The technical costs, such as training personnel in the collection, processing and analysis of data, have tended to be borne by the research teams (for example, the CBMS Network Coordinating Team, based at the Angelo King Institute for Economics and Business Studies, provides these services). The communities themselves also make valuable contributions by collecting and validating data.

The per-household cost of carrying out CBMS is considerably lower than the cost of surveys carried out by national statistical offices. For example, CBMS costs only around US$0.30 per household in Vietnam and US$0.75 in the Philippines. In addition to human and financial considerations, the most important element for CBMS implementation is the commitment of local government and other stakeholders to undertake the census and use the data generated.

CBMS around the world

As the CBMS network has spread from its base in the Philippines, it has supported research to develop indicators relevant to local cultures and conditions in different countries and regions, to adapt monitoring and analysis methodologies, and to develop case studies of vulnerable groups. Research teams have tested the application of new tools such as GIS (geographic information systems) to present CBMS data in map form.

As Part 3 of this book illustrates, all the countries now participating in the IDRC-supported CBMS network share common objectives, principles, and processes. However, the system has been adapted to reflect local conditions and capabilities, resulting in differences in questionnaires, coverage, processing systems, and uses. Some of these differences reflect the varying capacity in each country, as well as political and socio-economic conditions.

By bringing together the various elements described here and grounding them at the local level, CBMS has emerged as an innovative system. It has also set new standards in methodological rigour through the process of verifying data collected — and interpreting that data — with the communities. In doing this, the CBMS technical team facilitated understanding between communities and planners, government officials and policymakers of the important issues and prevailing conditions.

This is perhaps the most significant difference between CBMS and other poverty-monitoring approaches: the system is not only designed to satisfy the growing demand for up-to-date disaggregated information at the household level, but is also intended to be "institutionalized" at the lowest levels of government — the level that actually designs and implements many of the programs intended to address poverty. It also effectively promotes a system of "evidence-based" policy planning and decision-making.

Part 3

Experiences from the field

"People living in poverty have the least access to power to shape policies — to shape their future. But they have the right to a voice. They must not be made to sit in silence as 'development' happens around them, at their own expense. True development is impossible without the participation of those concerned."

— Nelson Mandela, Speech on receiving the Ambassador of Conscience Award 2006, Johannesburg, November 1, 2006

On the web
THE RESEARCH

As shown in Parts 1 and 2, CBMS developed as a unique poverty-monitoring system, specifically designed to collect and analyze information at the local level for use principally by local authorities in diagnosing the extent of poverty, planning and budgeting development programs, and assessing these programs' impact. CBMS emerged from the realization that finely targeted poverty-reduction interventions can best be achieved through understanding and applying individual and household information about the poor, involving communities with local governments, and ensuring political commitment for inclusive development. CBMS initiatives are therefore as much about improving local governance and empowering communities as they are about facilitating planning and resource allocation.

The examples that follow show that CBMS grew out of a process of interaction between local researchers, policymakers, and communities, adapted to specific on-the-ground conditions in different contexts, regions, and countries. It emerged as a localized data system for use in planning poverty reduction and other public sector programs at the local level, and not as simply a survey of the poor. Its community-level census approach to monitoring, however, also challenges its institutionalization as a national program, including the capacity-building required for local governments to scale-up the system and its integration with national poverty-monitoring systems.

Table 2. CBMS country partners and status of projects

Country	Year started	CBMS coverage area*
Philippines	1994	52 provinces (26 of which implement it province-wide), 531 municipalities, and 42 cities: a total of 13 498 *barangays*
Nepal	1996	Pilot communities in the Kavre, Dhanusha, Bardiya, Dailekh, and Jumla districts
Burkina Faso	1997	Village communities in the departments (divisions) of Yako and Diébougou
Vietnam	1997	Communes in the provinces of Ha Tay, Ninh Binh, Yen Bai, Quang Ngai, and Lam Dong
Sri Lanka	1998	Villages in the Hambantota and Batticaloa districts, and a municipality in Colombo
Senegal	2000	Communes and municipalities in Dakar, the Thiès region, and Diourbel
Bangladesh	2003	Communities in the Comilla District
Cambodia	2003	Communes from the provinces of Battambang, Kratie, and Kampong Thom
Lao PDR	2004	Villages in Sepone and Toumlan districts
Ghana	2004	Communities in the Dangme West District of the Greater Accra Region
Indonesia	2005	Communities in the Cianjur and Demak districts, in West and Central Java, and in Pekalongan
Benin	2005	Communities in the districts of Cotonou and Adogbe
Tanzania	2006	Communities in the Kndege Ward
Kenya	2007	Communities in the Tana River District
Zambia	2007	Communities in the Makishi and Mungule districts

As of January 2009.

The CBMS implemented in different countries (Table 2) share core elements. Each, however, reflects an adaptation to local needs and conditions as well as to the broader political, economic, and social environment.

ASIA

Philippines: From cradle to national implementation

CBMS results led to the establishment of Task Force Clean and Green and a health patrol to address health and nutrition problems. A health centre was constructed; a supplemental feeding program for children was introduced; toilets were distributed to households to improve the sanitation problem.

In January 2005, the National Statistical Coordination Board officially endorsed CBMS as a tool to strengthen the statistical system at the local level and directed its technical staff to promote the adoption of CBMS by Local Government Units (LGUs). In early February 2006, the Philippines' National Anti-Poverty Commission announced that it was adopting CBMS nation-wide. This welcome news followed similar directives by the Department of the Interior and Local Government that LGUs should adopt the CBMS core poverty indicators for poverty monitoring and planning.

By January 2009, CBMS was being implemented in 52 of the country's 81 provinces, including 531 municipalities and 42 cities, totalling 13 498 *barangays*. The goal: 100% coverage by 2010, the target date for the national implementation of a core local poverty indicators monitoring system.

Starting in Palawan

The story of how CBMS evolved in the Philippines starts in the province of Palawan. One of the hurdles provincial officials faced when they began to plan the 1999 budget was a lack of detailed municipal, village, household, and individual level information. This led officials to the CBMS developed through the IDRC-funded MIMAP-Philippines project.

Following a joint assessment of the province's data needs and availability by the CBMS research team and the Provincial Planning and Development Office (PPDO), provincial Governor Salvador Socrates issued an executive order for the creation of CBMS technical working groups within local governments, setting the stage for its institutionalization throughout the province. After pilot testing in two *barangays* of the Municipality of Taytay, the system went province-wide in 2000.

The strategy for implementing CBMS was based on partnership and resource-sharing, coordinated by provincial and municipal governments. Enumerators were recruited from the *barangays* and trained by the PPDO. After the household census was completed, PPDO staff returned to train community representatives in processing survey results. Municipal planning officers consolidated the data, while the CBMS team provided overall technical guidance and training for the provincial and municipal trainers, with support from IDRC. The cost for the first round of the survey amounted to only PhP 5.03 million (US$100 265), or US$1.42 per household. A substantial portion of this cost was for capacity building, the demand for which will decrease in subsequent rounds. The provincial government shouldered 13% of the cost; participating municipal governments provided the rest.

Improving the systems

The first round yielded valuable lessons about the types of questions asked and how they were phrased, which subsequent rounds helped to address. The validation process proved to be a particularly useful step in assessing the accuracy of the data as well as learning how communities understood the causes of poverty. CBMS implementation was most effective where municipal governments assumed a strong coordination role and where orientation, enumeration, and processing were carried out within a short time frame: delays reduced quantity and quality of the data and added to the cost.

Data processing was more difficult. Since many areas in Palawan had limited or no access to electricity, processing was done manually in the *barangays* and municipalities. The training was initially inadequate for those who were doing data processing for the first time and, for many, processing the local language questionnaire into English proved difficult. This led, in some cases, to processing having to be done by PPDO staff.

In spite of these difficulties, this first experience demonstrated the value of CBMS to the government. The provincial government used the CBMS data to prepare Palawan's first *Human Development Report* (2001). Municipal governments used the data to prepare their annual investment plans and to prioritize projects for poverty reduction, including investments on rural infrastructure, water supply and sanitation, and health and education services. Furthermore, the very precise information helped local governments evaluate the impacts of some of their projects.

A notable innovation in Palawan was the integration of geographic information systems (GIS) to present CBMS data in the form of easy-to-understand colour-coded maps that show each household in the community (Figure 2). GIS proved extremely instrumental to CBMS not only in depicting the poverty situation graphically but also as a tool to communicate with communities and policymakers.

The poverty maps are colour-coded representations of the poverty indicators. Unlike poverty maps generated from small area estimates (such as estimates for municipalities from national sample surveys that are designed to generate estimates for higher levels of aggregation), the CBMS maps show the poverty situation starting from the household level. By aggregating the household level data, estimates of poverty indicators are also generated. Poverty maps are then produced, portraying the poverty situation of the villages, municipalities, or provinces. With the colour-coded maps, policymakers can prioritize areas and households when delivering programs.

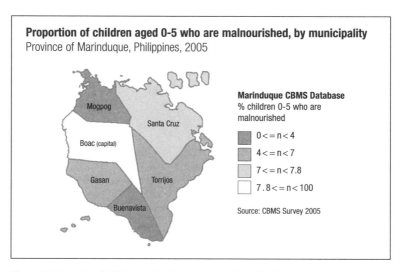

Proportion of children aged 0-5 who are malnourished, by municipality
Province of Marinduque, Philippines, 2005

Mogpog

Santa Cruz

Boac (capital)

Gasan

Torrijos

Buenavista

Marinduque CBMS Database
% children 0-5 who are malnourished

$0 <= n < 4$

$4 <= n < 7$

$7 <= n < 7.8$

$7.8 <= n < 100$

Source: CBMS Survey 2005

Figure 2. Example of GIS-generated maps presenting CBMS data (colours have been altered for this publication). The software used to generate these maps was the Natural Resource Database (NRDB) freeware, developed by a British Voluntary Services Overseas co-operant (Richard Alexander), customized to suit CBMS data (www.nrdb.co.uk). It is now an integral component of CBMS.

For example, when poverty maps were presented during a provincial planning convention, the head of municipal planning and development office in Bataraza, Palawan commented that the data on access to sanitation facilities by households seemed to be very low, as the municipality had recently carried out a latrine-distribution program in partnership with the national Department of Health. But when the municipal planner returned to the town to verify the CBMS survey results, he discovered that the latrines were distributed but not installed: the households were supposed to install them and contribute the cement and labour. Unfortunately, this had not been done and the latrines were never used. As a result, the program was redesigned to ensure that public investments into sanitation were properly used.

The successful implementation of CBMS in Palawan led to successive rounds in 2002, 2005, and a fourth in 2008. The information allowed planners to assess whether policies, programs, and projects implemented to address the problems were yielding the intended results, and whether living conditions were improving. For example, the provincial government became aware of the low school participation rate. This prompted them to examine more closely the issue of access to basic education and the quality of education being provided. In June 2006, the Palawan Regional Development Council reported that "CBMS has greatly benefited the province of Palawan," including helping to establish computerized databanks in almost all municipalities.

CBMS data has also been used for other planning purposes. In 2005, for example, the provincial government of Palawan prepared a poverty map of the entire province, in collaboration with the Peace and Equity Foundation and the Palawan Network of NGOs Inc. The National Red Cross in Puerto Princesa used the data to select sites for its Integrated Community Disaster Planning Program and to identify health and sanitation needs in communities.

Spread and evolution
From Palawan, CBMS spread to other provinces and is now in the process of being scaled-up up nation-wide. The costs of implementation have been largely borne by local governments, a

clear indication that they see the value of the system. Other stake-holders have also contributed, which bodes well for sustainability.

The growth of CBMS in the Philippines has been accompanied by adaptations to local circumstances. The CBMS team has assisted local governments in identifying and developing indicators specific to their communities — on migration, environmental protection, business-related activities, and natural disasters, among others. Similarly, the data collection and processing tools and training modules (in English and Tagalog) have been customized, resulting in four sets of household profile questionnaires and computerized processing systems incorporating specific local government concerns.

The CBMS team also developed a computerized national repository system, installed at the National Anti-Poverty Commission and the League of Municipalities of the Philippines. This repository houses all the CBMS data collected by the local governments and assists the Commission in its mandate of coordinating poverty-reduction policies and programs. The League can now use municipal-level data to identify and address inter-municipal concerns.

As the system has spread, so have the benefits. In *barangay* Kalamunding, Labo, for example, CBMS results led to the establishment of Task Force Clean and Green and a health patrol to address health and nutrition problems. A health centre was constructed; a supplemental feeding program for children was introduced; and toilets were distributed to households to improve the sanitation problem. A scholarship program was also launched to enable deserving students to finish their education. As significant, the *barangay*'s village captain (Constancia Labios) reported that attitudes also changed: CBMS has "prodded the parents in the community to attend to the health needs of their children such that more children aged 0–5 years are no longer malnourished."

The changes engendered by the information provided by CBMS to government officials and communities have further been reflected in policy and planning. As a 2004 review of the MIMAP program commissioned by IDRC noted, "Local officials have acknowledged that the community-based monitoring system made possible by MIMAP has helped depoliticize and strengthen the local government's budget allocation process by providing an objective basis for budget prioritization" (Saumier et al. 2004).

Rural to urban migration

CBMS has also found a home in the Philippines' crowded cities. Pasay City, for example, pilot tested CBMS in 2004 and became the first city in the national capital region to adopt it in its program planning and budgeting cycle. The indicators and questionnaires were customized to include data on the victims of crime and the number of persons with disabilities, as well as on the number of households with family members working overseas.

The city partnered with church-based NGOs to implement the CBMS "to preserve the integrity and transparency of the data collected," says Mayor Wenceslao Trinidad. In 2005, CBMS was conducted throughout the city's 201 *barangays*. Among the findings was a noticeable mismatch between labour supply and the types of employment available. A number of measures were subsequently taken to remedy the problem, including a public–private–civil society partnership to inventory skills and promote jobs and city-sponsored job fairs.

Spreading the word

The CBMS team based at the Angelo King Institute has been guiding the replication and adaptation throughout the country. As CBMS has grown, the team has been able to draw a number of lessons about what conditions need to exist for the system to root itself in the community, and how it can best be carried out. These are summarized in Part 4 of this book.

The Filipino experiences with developing and implementing CBMS have been well documented and disseminated. Advocacy is a critical component. Publications, digitized maps, databoards, a computerized database, an online database, meetings, and forums are just some of the tools used by the research team, collaborating agencies, and communities themselves.

Evidence-based program design, implementation, and monitoring have continued to be promoted through the CBMS Development Grant Program, launched in 2005. This program provides funds to local governments and NGOs to undertake interventions that address development needs identified through CBMS surveys. Funded by the United Nations Development Programme–Philippines and the Peace and Equity Foundation, the program has awarded 25 grants to date.

Vietnam: Focusing on basic needs in communes

Among those plans and programs have been vocational training in such areas as traditional crafts to generate employment, particularly for women, assistance to improve inadequate housing, and the provision of tools and agricultural inputs to boost food production.

Standing in the yard of her modest home on the edge of rice fields in Dai-Yen commune in Chuong-My district of Ha Tay province, a villager displays her poverty certificate. It attests that she is poor — or rather, that she is poorer than her neighbours in this farming community of close to 5 000 people on the outskirts of Hanoi. The card entitles this widowed mother of two to free health care, preferential loans, and other services. It is a valuable entitlement. Her right to the certificate was identified by other commune members — and by the CBMS piloted here.

This commune and others in the province serve as poverty observatories. Here, researchers have been working with the Managing Office of Vietnam's National Program on Hunger Eradication and Poverty Reduction (HEPR) and the Provincial Department of Labour, Invalids and Social Affairs (DOLISA) to implement CBMS.

Vietnam, once one of the poorest countries in the world, has made impressive strides in reducing poverty. The country now has one of the fastest economic growth rates in the world, averaging around 8% annually, and has emerged as a global exporter of many commodities and manufactures. The impact of Vietnam's economic policy reforms over the past decade and its rapid integration into the global economy has significantly improved living standards, bringing new wealth and uplifting the poor. According to the Vietnam Living Standard Surveys conducted by the General Statistics Office, the poverty rate dropped from 58.1% in 1993 to 20% in 2004.

The number of poor was more than halved during that same period but, says Vu Tuan Anh, Vice-Director of the Socio-Economic Development Centre, the country still has to overcome many challenges. There are significant regional disparities (notably between the cities and rural mountainous regions) and the gap between the haves and have-nots has increased. To meet Vietnam's MDG of halving the number of people living below the poverty line by 2010 and reducing by 75% those living under the food poverty line, two national programs have been launched: the National Target Program of Poverty Reduction 2006–2010 and the Program for Socio-Economic Development in Ethnic Minority and Mountainous Regions. But, says Vu Tuan Anh, identifying the poor for these programs, and evaluating their progress and success, requires reliable information (Vu 2007).

Most of the information on the poor in Vietnam is generated by national level surveys, such as the biennial Household Living Standards Survey (HLSS). Separately, poverty assessments have

On the web
THE RESEARCH

been carried out through the Ministry of Labour, Invalids and Social Affairs (MOLISA) and its provincial departments (DOLISA) at the commune level, as well as through various social organizations. These assessments have been largely on the basis of income, have been fairly subjective, and have not been comparable.

While these surveys offer good information at an aggregate level for the central government, they are not appropriate for planning poverty interventions and allocating resources at subnational levels of government. And because of the lack of reliable poverty estimates at local levels, schemes have been formed by different communities and social organizations — such as the Women's Union and Farmers' Union — for targeting the poor in their different locales. These have been uncoordinated and unreliable, however. Moreover, says Vu Tuan Anh, frequent changes in personnel in commune administrations and social organizations have meant that records have not been systematically kept.

Complementing data sources

Obtaining accurate, detailed data is the goal of the community-based poverty-monitoring system that Vu Tuan Anh and his research team have been developing since 1996 with IDRC support. The research team developed and tested a poverty-monitoring method based on simple indicators, short question-naires, and participatory techniques. Local staff carried out the survey, which combined quantitative and qualitative methods: the questionnaire and indicators were combined with group discussions and interviews with key informants. Results were analyzed using simple data-processing software.

Some of the initial results were surprising. In a commune of Lam Dong province, for instance, researchers found that only half of the poor households were receiving the credit to which they were entitled under the poverty-alleviation program, and that they were using it to meet basic consumption needs, such as food, and not for longer term production-oriented poverty reduction activities as intended (Asselin and Vu 2005).

The research concluded that poverty monitoring in Vietnam's rural areas should incorporate measures on basic needs rather than only on income and expenditure measures, be understandable and useful to a wide range of local users, and be participatory. In fact, viewed in the context of Vietnam's long tradition of community participation, the researchers found that CBMS created opportunities for local communities to define their poverty as well as to participate in reduction efforts.

The initial research led to CBMS being implemented to monitor a poverty-alleviation project in 30 communes of Thanh Hoa province. This project was supported by the Canadian International Development Agency (CIDA) and the government of Thanh Hoa province, and was carried out by CECI, based in Québec, Canada.

Subsequently, in cooperation with the research team, the Managing Office of the national HEPR program selected a set of poverty observatories in 20 communes of 12 provinces to pilot test the CBMS. The data enabled a detailed picture to be drawn of poor households. The results were also used to assess government poverty-reduction programs such as healthcare provision, education, housing, and credit. The Managing Office of the HEPR found that the CBMS baseline data would help assess the implementation of future poverty-reduction policies.

Increasing coverage

From this base, CBMS spread to different geographical and socio-economic regions of Vietnam, including to 30 commune observatories in all 13 districts of Ha Tay province and 10 commune observatories in eight districts of Yen Bai province. Elsewhere, the Women's Union of Ninh Binh province implemented CBMS in 27 communes of the poor, mountainous Nho Quan district. Five communes in Quang Nai, a province in Vietnam's central coastal

On the web
THE RESEARCH

region, are implementing CBMS. And, in Lam Dong, a province of the southern Central highlands where most of the population belongs to ethnic minorities, seven communes are using CBMS.

Indicators in Vietnam cover the community situation, household living standards, and the implementation of poverty-reduction policies and programs. As Vu Tuan Anh points out, indicators can be modified to reflect local needs. In Ninh Binh province, for instance, indicators were added on education, employment, the participation of women in social activities, and household decision-making.

"Because of this census, we have information we have never had before," says Le Thanh Trinh, chairman of the Gia Son Commune Administration in the very poor Nho Quan district. "Based on this data we can make plans." Among those plans and programs has been vocational training to generate employment, particularly for women, assistance to improve inadequate housing, and the provision of tools and agricultural inputs to boost food production.

Vu Tuan Anh points out that provincial authorities responsible for implementing poverty-reduction programs have benefited greatly from the CBMS results. The collected data has been used to assess poverty, evaluate poverty reports received from communes, and monitor the implementation of policies and programs of the National Targeted Program of Poverty Reduction. Several provinces are now requesting technical assistance to implement CBMS. And recently, questionnaires and indicators were adjusted to facilitate reporting on the MDGs: the national indicators now also include child mortality, mothers' health, and the incidence of HIV/AIDS, among other diseases, and draw on CBMS data sets.

Bangladesh: From research to practice

The information gathered helped to identify those who should benefit from public programs.

A low-income country, Bangladesh has about 144 million poor citizens, the third largest concentration in the world. While the economy has grown and livelihoods improved over the past decade, it has a considerable way to go to meet its objective of reducing poverty. The country's poverty profile reveals areas of extreme poverty as well as growing inequalities. Its 2005 Poverty Reduction Strategy Paper (PRSP) called for a more detailed multi-dimensional monitoring system taking in the ground realities that are useful for policymakers and planners.

"Poverty has always been on the government's agenda," says Mustafa Mujeri, former leader of the IDRC MIMAP-Bangladesh project, launched in 1992 by the Bangladesh Institute of Development Studies. One objective of that project was to strengthen the country's ability to monitor poverty. As Mujeri explained, poverty data in Bangladesh focused almost exclusively on income and consumption. Surveys were carried out infrequently — every 5 to 10 years. And more than 5 years could lapse between data collection and dissemination.

Working with the Bangladesh Bureau of Statistics (BBS) — the only national systematic data source in the country — the MIMAP research team met with various government departments, civil society, and other researchers to develop a multi-dimensional core set of 12 poverty indicators. Data was collected in 21 districts throughout the country. The indicators were refined and adjusted over the life of the project, including increased gender disaggregation.

The research team sought to find ways of ensuring that the data could be collected, processed, and delivered to policymakers in the shortest time and in forms they could easily understand. Training programs helped develop the capacity of BBS to collect process and verify data. Overall, it was found that the MIMAP poverty-monitoring system indicators provided deeper measures of poverty than those previously available. The effort paid off: MIMAP's poverty-monitoring survey data was used to prepare Bangladesh's PRSP. It also influenced budgetary allocations, increasing the percentage allocated to the social sector.

Involving communities

As communities and local governments became involved in monitoring poverty, the MIMAP poverty-monitoring system evolved into a community-based approach known as the Local-Level Poverty-Monitoring System (LLPMS). Pilot-tested in 2002–2003 in four villages of a Union Parishad, the system had three major components: participatory poverty and development monitoring; resource profile monitoring; and village development planning.

The pilot test was carried out by the Bangladesh Institute of Development Studies and the Bangladesh Academy for Rural Development, a national training and action-research institution under the Ministry of Local Government, Rural Development, and Cooperatives. Local institutions and the community actively participated in the process, and trained local youths collected the information from households.

Local officials and villagers collaborated with each other to identify and prioritize problems in an information book for each village, while the research team provided technical assistance. The information was shared with villagers and a ward information book was developed, setting out both village and household data and prioritizing identified problems. The villagers recognized the usefulness of the system and started using it to pressure higher levels of government to deliver better public services.

The trial enabled researchers to identify a number of challenges. First and foremost, these included mobilizing local people and obtaining local government support (a prerequisite for sustaining the process). To ensure the quality of data — and the collaboration of all households — the team found that enumerators needed to be of different professions, ages, and gender, and from different socio-economic groups. The questionnaire needed to be kept simple and cross-checked through focus group discussions, and carried out during the slack agricultural season to allow sufficient time for interviews (Mujeri and Guha 2006).

The success of the pilot test led to its replication the following year in all villages of Muhammadpur Union (West), under the Daudkandi Upazila of Comilla District. Local government representatives and villagers were trained to analyze the information and to identify and prioritize problems to develop a pragmatic plan. Ward meetings were held to disseminate findings.

Villagers were motivated by the information — new to them, they said — to organize to fight poverty. The result was that representatives from neighbouring Union Parishad asked that the LLPMS be implemented in their areas and representatives of the National Statistics Department be involved in the process.

On the web
THE RESEARCH

Linking research to practice
The lessons from Bangladesh are consistent with those from the Philippines and Vietnam:

➤ Support and training need to be provided to local people in collecting and tabulating data.

➤ The systems' sustainability rests on the involvement of governments.

➤ Governments at all levels, as well as other agencies, need to participate to ensure the wide use of the data.

➤ Linking the CBMS and national indicators helps sensitize policymakers.

➤ Indicators and questionnaires need to be simple and short.

The researchers also found that information dissemination by the local government officials was instrumental in mobilizing people. Says Ranjan Kumar Guha, the Academy's assistant director and CBMS-Bangladesh project leader, "Incorporating some household data in the village information book helps to ensure the quality of the data because villagers go to check what is recorded about them." Local authorities also noted that the information gathered helped to identify those who should benefit from public programs such as government-issued vulnerable group feeding cards (Guha 2006).

Academy researchers have been actively promoting the LLPMS through a series of workshops. But institutionalizing the system in Bangladesh is a long-term process requiring the commitment of union-level officials as well as NGOs and community representatives in partnership with the research community and higher levels of government.

Cambodia: Improving local statistics and governance

When the survey in Kbal Snoul village showed how many children did not attend school because none was accessible, a donor stepped forward to build a new school within walking distance.

Reducing poverty is a pressing need in Cambodia where more than 35% of the population lives under the poverty line of US$0.50 a day. The country is also committed to the process of decentralization to make the provision of public services more responsive and more effective to citizens' needs. As part of this process, 1 621 communes were established as legal entities, governed by councils first elected in 2002, to be responsible for local development planning and implementation.

As Try Sothearith, deputy director of the National Institute of Statistics' (NIS) Department of Demographic Statistics, Census and Survey, notes, "Commune councils need adequate information, generated in a systematic and reliable way, in order to effectively conduct their needs assessments, planning, monitoring, and evaluation of development projects" (Sothearith et al. 2006). At the time, commune databases existed, but the information they contained was largely garnered from administrative reports completed by the village chief without household visits. Moreover, the databases, set up under the SEILA program (a joint government–donor program to promote local planning and development in support of decentralization), were to close at the program's end in 2006.

In 2003, the Cambodia Development Resource Institute, in collaboration with the National Institute and the Seila program, piloted a CBMS in six communes in two provinces. To meet the goal of creating a sustainable system to locally monitor poverty over time, the project emphasized institutional capacity building at the local level.

Drawing on the experience of other Southeast Asian countries where CBMS had been established, and with the assistance of the CBMS Network Coordinating Team from the Angelo King Institute in the Philippines, a core set of nine indicators was developed.

The CBMS developed in Cambodia involved all levels of government. School teachers and other knowledgeable villagers were recruited and trained as enumerators. Village chiefs worked with the enumerators in listing households and mapping villages. Commune councils supervised the survey teams and data processing, helping to ensure their buy-in. District and provincial statistical offices handled data cleaning and coding as well as data entry. Finally, the research team from the National Institute of Statistics analyzed the data, wrote reports, and disseminated the results.

The project yielded valuable results in terms of adequately describing the different facets of poverty in the pilot communes and in building the capacities of local authorities. According to CBMS project leader Sothearith, "The pilot project successfully promoted links between the commune, provincial, and national level planning processes." And, as important, the project "built the capacities of local authorities to implement and take responsibility to upgrade CBMS in their localities."

Broadening the reach

Results of the pilot project were widely shared and NIS carried out a second round survey of 12 communes in 2006. Because most of Cambodia's rural areas lack electricity and processing had to be done manually, one district officer introduced the use of a second-hand computer powered by a car battery. This small innovation enabled commune officers to process data electronically in even the most remote areas.

The CBMS survey results were widely disseminated and used by commune councilors, local development partners, and by other line ministries and development organizations. For example, when the survey in Kbal Snoul village showed how many children did not attend school because none was accessible, a donor stepped forward to build a new school within walking distance. The information also led to other investments. Two roads were built to link the village to the main road, saving villagers a 45-minute walk on a narrow path. Discovering the high number of households that were landless led to a program to allocate them public land.

In fact, participating communes noted that the CBMS results were an excellent tool for attracting donor assistance as they provided an accurate picture of the community's needs. "CBMS is a clear measurement tool," says one village councillor. "No other instrument provides actual rates. No one can challenge this data." Survey results have also enabled communities to better deal with their own problems. For instance, the relatively high number of cases of domestic violence in one village has led to education and deterrence programs for offenders. Bringing the problem out into the open has led to a dramatic reduction in cases of violence.

The success of CBMS in Cambodia has led to considerable demand from both policymakers and local government planners for scaling up. The NIS is planning for the next round during which the coverage will extend to all the communes in three more districts, with the intent to cover one entire province. This has also generated interest among other provincial governors and development organizations. The main drawback, however, is low absorptive capacity and a shortage of external technical and financial assistance.

In an effort to address these constraints, H.E. San Sy Than, NIS' director-general, has proposed that a CBMS bureau be established within the Institute to promote CBMS throughout the country and to build capacity among statistical officers and local communes. This would greatly assist the implementation of Cambodia's 2005 *Statistics Law*, which also proposes that an NIS planning officer be placed in every commune in the country.

On the web
THE RESEARCH

Lao PDR: Bottom-up data collection and poverty targeting

The CBMS provided the most reliable base from which to start socio-economic development planning and has been used to improve the targeting of poverty alleviation projects.

Nearly one-third of the Laotian population is estimated to live in poverty. Many of the poor live in isolated regions and comprise numerous distinct ethnic groups with special needs. In the Laotian context, poverty is understood differently by different cultural groups: understanding culture and social structure is therefore important to meet the needs of the poor. The Government of Lao PDR has thus put considerable emphasis on "people-centred" development and improving "livelihoods" in its national effort to meet its MDG objectives and move out of its "least developed country" status.

To reach the goal of achieving the MDGs by 2015 and becoming a lower middle income country by 2020, the Lao PDR government adopted a National Growth and Poverty Eradication Strategy in 2001. The National Statistics Centre (NSC) was charged with poverty monitoring and analysis in the strategy's framework. Implementing and monitoring it, however, requires detailed information about the poor. The strategy indicated that further disaggregating poverty information and analysis would help identify pro-poor policy actions (see World Bank 2006). It further acknowledged the importance of building capacity.

The approach taken by NSC was bottom-up, drawing from community-collected data to bolster national databases. To obtain this information, NSC introduced a decentralized system of Village Book Statistics in 2004 — a community-level demographic and socio-economic statistical database — to complement the Lao

Expenditure and Consumption survey to monitor poverty at the national level.

In implementing the Village Book system, however, NSC realized that a crucial step was missing: villagers were asked to aggregate data into the book but did not have any tools to collect data at the household level. Statistical capacity in Lao PDR was also weak at all levels. To address this problem, NSC pilot-tested CBMS in four villages of two districts. By 2005 it was extended to 24 villages in two provinces in the country's poorest districts. In addition to providing timely information, the project was intended to facilitate the country's decentralization efforts by directly involving people in the design of programs that best address their needs.

Through the project, NSC was able to develop an improved set of indicators to support the Village Book and inform local development activities, as well as corresponding data collection and processing instruments. The village enumerators were trained to collect, compile, and validate the data. Training was also provided in data entry, processing, and tabulation. The low level of education and weak statistical and computer skills of enumerators proved challenging and necessitated longer training than anticipated. The data was shared at the local level and with all statisticians in the provinces. The results were also disseminated in national forums.

According to Phosy Keosiphandone, deputy director general, Department of Planning and Investment of Saravan Province, CBMS provided the most reliable base from which to start socio-economic development planning and has been used to improve the targeting of poverty-alleviation projects and resource allocation. In addition to yielding fundamental information at the village level on the poor for planning purposes, CBMS was invaluable in other respects. It provided evidence for policymakers to better understand the ground realities of the different communities and thus helped to prioritize public sector programs. The system strengthened capacity at the local level, as well as within NSC, and the involvement of communities greatly enhanced their own understanding of development programs, giving them a sense of ownership. It also helped to improve coordination between the NSC and local officials in planning.

Private investors, NGOs, and donors in Lao PDR have found that the CBMS data-enriched Village Books reduced the need for additional surveys in planning their programs. As Keosiphandone (2007) notes, the data explained discrepancies between improving incomes and stagnant poverty levels. "Interestingly, we found in the first year that one village had a high increase in income, but at the end of the second year the income poverty level had not declined. They spent most of their income on alcohol and satellite TV." This helped local planners better understand local behaviour and views of poverty.

Indonesia: Tailoring CBMS to multi-dimensional indicators

Ensuring local ownership of the system and data, this initiative is fully supported by local government officials, including the mayor and his deputy.

Reforms in Indonesia have had an important positive impact on the poor, and include its system of decentralized government, which has sought to bring services closer to the people. However, despite significant strides in reducing overall poverty, close to 42% of Indonesians still live between the US$1 and $2 a day poverty lines, underlining the high vulnerability of many to falling into deeper poverty and the need to closely monitor the situation. More attention also needs to be paid to non-income multi-dimensional measures, such as malnutrition rates, access to safe drinking water, sanitation, and so on. There are considerable regional disparities and growing inequalities — all of which point to the need for disaggregated data for planning.

Indonesia's decentralized planning structure and regional autonomy have given local governments responsibilities to implement development activities for their constituencies. When local governments needed to identify the poor to better target poverty reduction programs, they turned to the National Family Planning Coordination Board, the only national agency that annually collects household level data. Because the Board's data was intended solely to monitor family-planning programs, it proved inadequate for the task. Subsequent efforts by local governments proved costly and unsatisfactory, largely because of a weak methodology and training of personnel (Suryadarma et al. 2005).

In the quest to introduce a better poverty monitoring tool in Indonesia, the Lembaga Penelitian SMERU Research Institute proposed pilot-testing a CBMS in collaboration with the Board in four villages in Java. A set of locally specific proxy indicators of welfare was developed, which included items such as asset ownership, health characteristics, political participation, and access to information.

These were used to score families' welfare. To check the scores' robustness, the richest and poorest families were compared. The comparison showed that there was a wide gap between the two groups in almost all the indicators, in all villages. The test also found asset ownership variables to be the most significant welfare indicators. Education, health, and consumption patterns were also important, but the importance of each varied from village to village. This convinced researchers that local specificity in indicators is crucial in Indonesia given its large population, size, and heterogeneity.

The pilot test also showed that, with training and supervision, Board cadres and educated villagers could be effective enumerators — in fact, although their education level was important in ensuring accuracy, their level of enthusiasm was just as crucial a factor. Interestingly, and contrary to CBMS implementation elsewhere, the Indonesia team considers that "village officials should not be

On the web
THE RESEARCH

involved in order to ensure that data is not tampered with.... Village officials are more prone to making mistakes in data collection."

After successfully completing the pilot phase, SMERU started to train local governments interested in applying CBMS in their areas, with the expectation that the system can be institutionalized by local governments. The local government of the City of Pekalongan in Central Java was the first to plan to implement CBMS, starting in 2008, to support their poverty-reduction programs. With assistance from SMERU, it is collecting data on the socio-economic status of the community and will use it to better plan and budget. This project covers the entire city, consisting of 4 *kecamatan* (sub-districts) and 46 *kelurahan* (villages), with a population of 320 000 divided into some 80 000 families. The coverage will effectively institutionalize CBMS in the city.

It is expected that the City of Pekalongan will be a model for CBMS institutionalization for other local governments in Indonesia. Ensuring local ownership of the system and data, this initiative is fully supported by local government officials, including the mayor and his deputy, who are serving as supervisors, and a technical team consisting of officials of the Regional Development Planning Board, Planning and Evaluation Division, and the Administrative Division.

Other CBMS initiatives in Asia

Pakistan
In the context of the Poverty Reduction Strategy Paper process, Pakistan introduced far-reaching policy commitments that stress decentralization and devolution of powers to local governments. The local government ordinances, which established new accountability arrangements giving local government responsibility for service delivery and the establishment of community

citizens boards, created new demands for local-level statistics and monitoring of public programs.

CBMS has been tested in Pakistan to provide an empirical base for budget allocation and planning within the local government. Researchers at the Pakistan Institute for Development Economics designed a core set of indicators to monitor and evaluate development policies and programs and presented it to national stakeholders. A customized set of data collection, processing, and validation tools was also developed and pilot-tested. Work focused on incorporating into CBMS as many indicators as possible from Pakistan's National Reconstruction Bureau's Information Management System.

While the administrative, political, and fiscal reforms supporting devolution proved conducive for CBMS to assist local governments in their planning and allocative responsibilities, political tensions and concomitant uncertainties and risks with partnerships between the research community, civil society, and various local government administrations and institutions have limited the development of CBMS.

Nepal

In Nepal, decentralization allowed local initiatives and development interventions to be conceived, designed, and implemented by Village Development Committees, the lowest government level. This created demand for local level information that was not provided by the Nepal Living Standards Survey, conducted every 5 years. Under a MIMAP project, the research team from the National Labour Academy launched an information-gathering system at the local level in 1997. Unlike other CBMS initiatives, however, the data was collected through focus group discussions rather than through household surveys. CBMS started to make some headway in Nepal's system of local government and decentralized planning, but work in many of the rural areas was interrupted by political conflict and was discontinued.

On the web
THE RESEARCH

Sri Lanka

Sri Lanka set a course for devolution with the creation of provincial councils and an elected local government structure consisting of village councils (*Pradeshiya Sabhas*), and municipal and urban councils. Local government institutions, however, were slow to develop and were hindered by political problems and conflict. They were also constrained by a lack of effective planning and development coordination. Nevertheless, the need for good data collection at the village level to support poverty reduction efforts remained. In response, the Social Policy Analysis and Research Centre at the University of Colombo undertook to pilot-test a CBMS in three locations in 2003.

The project yielded a detailed picture of the communities and confirmed the importance of locally relevant multi-dimensional indicators. The researchers concluded that although CBMS could become a valuable tool in Sri Lanka, it "can materialize only if a concerted effort is made to change the status quo" with respect to the lack of capability and empowerment within local governments (Hettige 2005). As CBMS project leader Siripala Hettige noted, "The persisting marginalisation of local government institutions within the Sri Lankan political system has been a hindrance to institutionalising CBMS within the local government framework in Sri Lanka" (Hettige 2007).

AFRICA

In October 2007, of the 41 countries eligible for relief under the Heavily Indebted Poor Countries (HIPC) initiative, 32 were in sub-Saharan Africa. Among them were Benin, Burkina Faso, Ghana, Senegal, Tanzania, and Zambia, countries where CBMS has been introduced. IDRC's MIMAP program supported teams in Benin, Burkina Faso, Ghana, and Senegal, starting in the late 1990s as part of an effort to rethink approaches to combating poverty. This work led some IDRC-supported researchers to collaborate in preparing their countries' Poverty Reduction

Strategy Papers (PRSPs). A key element in implementing the PRSP was the development of a monitoring and evaluation framework to track progress.

Burkina Faso: Empowering the poor

Since the survey, villagers have built retaining structures to capture rainwater for agriculture, thus increasing crops and reducing hunger.

The UNDP's 2007 *Human Development Report* ranks Burkina Faso number 176 out of 177 countries in its Human Development Index, an unenviable position. To provide impetus to the country's poverty-reduction efforts, Burkina Faso approved its first PRSP in 2000 and its second in 2004, the country's reference point for defining development programs and activities. Among the PRSP's main objectives are to build the capabilities of the poor and to implement strong partnerships with communities in poverty-reduction programs. Building local capacity to promote development at the community level and to reinforce local governance is also an integral element of Burkina Faso's decentralization program.

Burkina Faso became part of the MIMAP network in the mid-1990s. The research was carried out by the Centre d'Étude, de Documentation et de Recherche Économique et Sociale (CEDRES) of the University of Ouagadougou and the Institut National de la Statistique et de la Démographie (INSD). In the wake of similar projects in Asia, CEDRES and INSD undertook in 1997 to pilot test a CBMS in partnership with a Canadian NGO, the Centre d'étude et de coopération internationale. The goal: to develop a methodology and select indicators.

Decentralization, and later the PRSP, set the stage for the development of the CBMS and for bridging the gaps and deficiencies in effectiveness or efficiency of the country's development programs.

On the web
THE RESEARCH

Those gaps include a lack of current, disaggregated data, of involvement in development planning, of participation in decision-making, of coordination between various programs, and of local capacity, particularly in rural areas where 90% of the population is illiterate.

The need for revisions

A pilot test was carried out in 110 households in three areas — rural, semi-urban, and urban — of Passore province. Drawing from the CBMS indicators developed in the Philippines, the Burkina Faso team selected the most relevant for local circumstances. Because of large seasonal changes in the mainly agricultural population's living conditions, it was determined that data should be collected twice a year for some indicators, such as the use of healthcare facilities, once yearly for others.

The initial research showed that data-collection capacity in villages was weak. The existing tools and training manuals needed revision and more time had to be allocated to training. These were reflected in a second phase of research, launched in 2000. Among the new measures:

➤ community sensitization and training before the survey;

➤ the incorporation of a gender and development strategy to increase women's participation in designing and implementing the CBMS; and

➤ creating greater synergy with local development financing programs so that needs identified by the communities could be met.

In 2002, the system was tested in five villages and one urban sector in the department (administrative division) of Yako. In 2003, this was extended to cover the department's more than 73 000 people in 8 454 households. A controller supervised the work of locally selected and trained enumerators, while a central team ensured quality control. Data processing was done manually to respect the CBMS principle of community control and use. The research team helped aggregate and analyze the data electronically.

Because of the high level of illiteracy in the country, communicating the CBMS results back to the community posed a particular challenge. The solution: translate the data into easy-to-interpret drawings on paper and blackboards, one for each indicator — population size, health and nutrition, sanitation, education — posted at the village assembly offices (Figure 3). These drawings have also been used to illustrate handbooks and the information has been translated into Moore, a local language.

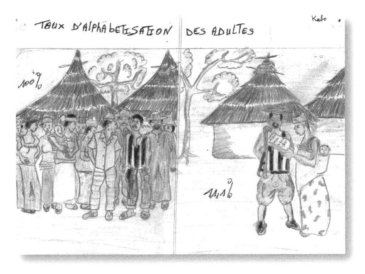

Figure 3. This poster illustrates an adult literacy rate of 11.1% in the village of Kabo.

The resulting detailed picture of poverty held up to the communities spurred some to action. In Lilbouré, for instance, the results galvanized the community into building retaining structures to capture rainwater for agriculture. As well, school enrolment more than doubled.

According to CBMS team leader Prosper Somda of CEDRES, CBMS is the only data collection tool that communities can use to develop evidence-based plans. Lilbouré wants to repeat the survey every 2 years but, says Somda, it does not have the resources or the expertise to do so on its own. And the computer skills needed for data analysis do not exist in the village.

In 2006, the team extended the CBMS to two new sites — the Departments of Diébougou and Koper, the latter at the request of Africa's Sustainable Development Council, a consortium of development organizations. In Diébougou, the success of a pilot project in 5 localities led to the decision to survey the entire commune close to 40 000 people in 23 villages to prove that CBMS was feasible and to convince national authorities of its value to complement the national statistical system. As in Yako, the survey results painted a sad picture: high rates of child mortality and low levels of medical care, a severe shortage of sanitary facilities, low levels of school attendance, particularly for girls, and precarious living conditions.

In Koper, the findings showed that "For all indicators, the Department of Koper suffers from numerous deficits that constitute great challenges for local authorities and other development actors" (Konate et al. 2007).

In late April 2008 the mayor of Yako, reported that the CBMS results had enabled him to negotiate funding for priority development projects. "Whoever has information is wealthy," he says. "I needed reliable data. I was working in the dark which made it difficult to obtain financing. The CBMS results are already being used to improve people's welfare."

Senegal: Supporting the PRSP

When village officials noted that schools were concentrated in the north of the village — and that children there were higher school achievers — they decided to build three new schools in underserved areas.

Two events were early stimulants for developing the CBMS program in Senegal. One was the passing in March 1996 of the decentralization law, which devolved economic and social development functions to local governments. The second event was the launch in 2001 of Senegal's PRSP process.

As part of the MIMAP Senegal project, Senegalese researchers worked closely with the government on the design of the PRSP. The team included researchers from the Centre de recherches économiques appliquées and from various units of the Ministry of Economy and Finance. However, Senegal did not have an adequate system to monitor households' living conditions. In October 2002, the Planning and Statistics Directorate led the development of an integrated system to monitor poverty, living conditions, and human development. A national observatory was set up to collect and analyze data and disseminate results that would be useful for local planning.

The CBMS Senegal team was tasked with developing and testing this system in three locations: Guédiawayé, a suburban Dakar commune; a semi-rural commune in Thiès region; and Ndangalma, a rural community in Diourbel. Local authorities in Guédiawayé confirmed their readiness to set up the system and to make available local personnel. In the rural commune of Ndangalma, inadequate access to services and markets had led to "a group dynamic among the local populations of participation in grass-roots leadership organizations for joint thinking and action to promote sustainable local development," says Momar Ballé Sylla, the CBMS Senegal coordinator.

On the web
THE RESEARCH

A vibrant civil society also existed in Tivaouane, Thiès. And, as in Guédiawaya, "the people have decided to take charge of their future," says Sylla. In addition — and perhaps not coincidentally for the selection of Tivaouane as a pilot site — the then newly elected mayor, El Hadj Malick Diop, was a statistician formerly employed by the Planning and Statistics Directorate.

Both Tivaouane and Guédiawaye passed administrative acts to institutionalize the monitoring systems. No decree was passed in Ndangalma, but the community president made the community secretaries available to the research team.

Two questionnaires were administered: one to communities and one to households. The first covered such indicators as demographic characteristics, education and literacy, health and nutrition, community organizations, economy, and infrastructure. The household questionnaire gathered data on household composition, education, health, employment, and international migration, in addition to living conditions. In 2003, a small sample of households was interviewed in each locality because, says Sylla, it would be too expensive to survey all households. The sample was selected in collaboration with the district commissioner or village leaders. All district and village leaders were also surveyed.

The surveyors were recruited from the community and chosen by the mayor or rural commune president. The training program included instruction, testing, and translation of parts of the questionnaires from French into local languages, and field observation. The process led to a revision of the training manual. Data processing was done electronically by locally recruited and trained personnel.

A case for community validation

The research team provided the compiled results to city officials who shared them with the community through workshops. While community responses were generally positive, some noted the absence of indicators on income and maternal and infant mortality. The accuracy of some figures, such as the estimated population in Ndangalma, was also questioned, forcing researchers to return to the survey files.

Some of the results astounded the residents of Tivaouane. For instance, they discovered that more than 52% of the population was unmarried, an anomaly in a very religious community. But, says Mayor Diop, this is a manifestation of poverty. "With very high unemployment and crowding of two, three, and even four people in each bedroom, life as a couple is virtually impossible," he says. When village officials noted that schools were concentrated in the north of the village — and that children there were higher school achievers — they decided to build three new schools in underserved areas.

The mayors of Tivaouane and Guédiawaye committed themselves to finance the collection of resources needed for a second phase and to expand coverage to other districts. Among others who expressed their intention to use the CBMS data were UNDP's poverty program and the NGO Enda Tiers Monde.

Although the value of the CBMS was evident through the pilots, local officials were unsure if communities' financial resources were adequate to cover the costs of future surveys. They also noted that additional training was needed for those charged with data analysis. Among other lessons learned was the need to sensitize households before the survey, to translate the questionnaires into local languages, to better adapt questionnaires to the locality, and to further validate the data collected.

CECI's Louis-Marie Asselin points out that the Senegal CBMS differs from other CBMS projects in that it has a very complex

On the web
THE RESEARCH

sampling design at the community level and is highly computerized, using three software programs to process and analyze data. The local government would need to have advanced capability in sampling and computer skills to adopt this system. Asselin further notes that the relatively small sample may not be sufficient to meet the needs of local development planning. The links with the national statistical system offer high potential for policy impact, however.

Sylla notes a number of challenges in the way of full-scale implementation of CBMS in Senegal:

→ obtaining the commitment and support of communities to introduce and finance their own CBMS;

→ ensuring the continued use of the data generated to evaluate the impact of development projects; and

→ maintaining relationships between stakeholders, particularly the Ministry of Social Development, local authorities, and villagers.

Benin: Strong municipal support

The mayor's office of the town of Cotonou announced six priority actions to improve living conditions…. All the measures proposed were identified through a CBMS survey.

In 2007, the mayor's office of the capital city of Cotonou announced six priority actions to improve living conditions in the city's 13th district. Topping the list: the provision of sewage, sanitary, and health facilities; the extension of electrical services and safe water supplies; and mosquito-control operations to combat malaria. All the measures proposed were identified through a CBMS survey carried out the previous year.

With a per capita income of US$540 in 2006 and a ranking of 163 out of 177 countries according to the 2007 UNDP *Human Development Report*, Benin remains a very poor country. Reducing poverty and accelerating economic growth is the government's priority, articulated in its PRSP. In addition, the government is pursuing a policy to improve public accountability and governance. But, as the Benin CBMS team notes, doing so requires the participation of communities at every step of implementation and monitoring.

In 2005, a team from the Université d'Abomey Calavi, supported by the Institut national de la statistique et de l'analyse économique, piloted a CBMS in the 13th district of Cotonou. In 2006, CBMS was extended to two other districts, Covè and Adjarra. To ensure that the data collected could be compared with national data sources, the team adopted the EMICoV (Enquête Modulaire Integrée sur les Conditions de Vie — integrated modular survey of household living conditions) questionnaire. The national EMICoV survey had been carried out in 2005. In total, 16 300 households were surveyed.

The CBMS aims to provide disaggregated data at the local level to support the country's decentralization process, which started in December 2004. Benin's Observatory of Social Change only monitors poverty and measures its impact at the national level.

Project leader Marie Odile Attanasso notes that the census highlighted great disparities in the communities surveyed. "The results urge the local authorities and the NGOs and development associations to come to the aid of the populations in order to improve their living standard and their living conditions," she writes (Attanasso 2007). This, Cotonou's municipal council took to heart. "This survey made it possible for the town council to give this district a real face," said Mayor Nicéphore Dieudonné Soglo (CBMS 2008).

On the web
THE RESEARCH

The mayor of Adjarra concurs: "This tool is very suitable to know the level of poverty of the town and to define the best strategies for poverty alleviation," he said. "So I promise to mobilize funds to expand the CBMS through the town after this first phase."

A number of challenges lie ahead, however, including a lack of human and financial resources and of statistical services at the local level, the low level of education of local authorities, and the unavailability of data-storage facilities.

From West to East Africa

In 2006, Kenya, Tanzania, and Zimbabwe joined the CBMS family. In Kenya, the system is intended to become an early warning system to monitor drought and ethnic conflict and to understand the relationship between the two. In Tanzania, the project complements the national government's efforts to achieve participatory planning and monitoring in the context of decentralization. In Zimbabwe, although constrained by political and economic circumstances, the system is building on the community monitoring program launched in 2003 and seeks to strengthen the links between community monitoring and community research. Zambia joined the network in 2007 in an effort to link data from local-level monitoring with decision-making for poverty reduction .

Conclusion

As these project descriptions demonstrate, CBMS has progressively made inroads throughout both Asia and Africa. By 2008, CBMS programs had spread to nine Asian countries. The extent of CBMS work is growing both in breadth and depth as more local governments adopt this approach to refine policies and programs to address the needs of the poor. Interest is also growing as efforts to "localize" MDG monitoring gain prominence.

Clearly, everywhere, "CBMS has not only permitted the acquisition of a richer body of information and data on the welfare of the poor in developing countries. It has also led to the almost serendipitous result of offering a way to empower poor local communities in asserting their needs to their local and national governments and in influencing budgetary allocations.... As such, CBMS has become much more than a research tool, turning into a direct instrument for empowerment and actual poverty reduction" (Habito et al. 2004).

Localizing the Millenium Development Goals through CBMS

In most countries, progress toward the MDGs is monitored at the national level. If they are to be achieved, however, there must be a parallel effort to bring the MDGs into the mainstream local development agenda. Unfortunately, however, national statistical systems have yet to respond adequately to the demand for micro-level statistics that can help local governments reduce poverty (World Bank 2005).

As the following examples show, the CBMS that is being implemented in a number of Asian and African countries is well positioned to track progress toward the MDGs at the local level. For one, a number of indicators being monitored in the CBMS are included in the indicators for monitoring progress toward the MDGs (Table 3). Moreover, as CBMS surveys are intended to be carried out on a regular basis: they can therefore be used to update MDG indicators and facilitate reporting. The CBMS can also help national and local governments to cost and identify appropriate interventions to achieve the MDGs and allocate resources.

The Philippines — In 2005, the National Statistical Coordination Board issued Resolution No. 6 "recognizing and enjoining support to the CBMS as a tool for strengthening the statistical system at the local level that will generate statistics for monitoring and evaluation of development plans, including the progress of the local governments in attaining the Millennium Development Goals."

Vietnam — Another track has been followed in Vietnam. It has assimilated the MDGs into its own national socio-economic development strategy by establishing 12 development goals (commonly referred to as Vietnam's Development Goals, or VDGs) and translating these into specific targets. However, although progress toward the VDGs is monitored at the national and provincial levels, the same is not being done at the local level, which may threaten the country's sustained gains in poverty reduction.

Indonesia — There is growing recognition in Indonesia that information on progress toward the MDGs at the national level masks the differing conditions at the local level, resulting in significant leakage and undercoverage in program delivery. CBMS-generated data is now being used in pilot sites to complement household-level data from the National Family Planning Coordination Board in identifying beneficiaries of poverty reduction and social protection programs.

Table 3. The MDGs and CBMS core indicators

MDG	CBMS core indicators
1. Eradicate extreme poverty and hunger	Proportion of households with income less than the poverty threshold
	Proportion of households with income below the food threshold
	Proportion of 0–5-year-old children who are moderately and severely underweight
	Proportion of households who eat less than three full meals a day
2. Achieve universal primary education	Proportion of 6–12-year-old children who are not in elementary school
	Proportion of 13–16-year-old children who are not in secondary school
3. Promote gender equality	Ratio of girls to boys in primary and secondary education
	Ratio of literate women to men
4. Reduce child mortality	Proportion of children under 5 years old who died
5. Improve maternal health	Proportion of women who died due to pregnancy-related causes
6. Combat HIV/AIDS, malaria, and other infectious diseases	Proportion of households without access to safe water
	Proportion of households without sanitary toilet facilities
7. Ensure environmental sustainability	Proportion of households who are squatters
	Proportion of households with makeshift housing
8. Develop a global partnership for development	Proportion of 15-year-olds and above who are not working but are actively seeking work

CBMS' role in localizing the MDGs was recognized during an Experts Group Meeting on Localizing the MDGs held November 28, 2006 at the United Nations Economic and Social Commission for Asia and the Pacific (UNESCAP) in Bangkok, Thailand. The Committee on Poverty Reduction composed of 24 nation states agreed that the CBMS could complement the official data collection activities of national statistical offices and improve the availability of MDG and other indicators at the local level. It also agreed that localizing the MDGs through CBMS would help integrate the goals into national development strategies. It therefore urged other developing countries to initiate and implement similar innovative systems to help localize the MDGs. As a result, the UNESCAP Asia Pacific Regional Roadmap identified CBMS as one of the tools to localize the MDGs.

The lessons learned from these experiences about the need for CBMS, its uses and benefits, and about the ways it can and should best be implemented, are presented in Part 4. These experiences have also shown the transformative power of a community-based process. CBMS is proving a good incubator for change agents. It is also an effective bridge between government and the people it serves.

Lessons and Recommendations

"Better use of better statistics leads to better policy and better development outcomes."

— *Christopher Scott, London School of Economics, January 2005*

The previous chapter briefly described the implementation of a number of CBMS initiatives in Asia and Africa. The scope and maturity of these programs vary, as do their prospects for institutionalization and sustainability. Most are ongoing and more continue to be launched, further adding to the CBMS experience.

The growth of CBMS has demonstrated that the need for disaggregated, community-level information is acute in many parts of the world. And demand is growing, in part to meet local-level planning requirements in support of decentralization and to implement targeted poverty interventions, and in part to monitor progress toward meeting benchmarks in anti-poverty and other public investment programs (such as PRSPs). The need to

On the web
THE LESSONS

measure progress toward meeting MDG commitments creates additional demand.

The overarching lesson from the research over the past decade is that designing and sustaining community-based poverty monitoring systems is an essential component of national poverty monitoring systems. The usual system based on national sample surveys does not provide all the information needed by policymakers. Our experience has shown that CBMS is feasible. With training, communities and local governments are able to implement the systems at an affordable cost.

Carried out at regular intervals, CBMS provides accurate disaggregated data that enables local government planners to effectively and efficiently target investments — with attention to gender and social equity considerations — and monitor progress. It also enables them to do so relatively easily in partnership with their constituencies. Furthermore, it gives communities a simple tool for holding governments accountable, thereby fostering good governance.

However, CBMS is not a panacea for statistical and planning challenges. It should be viewed as a complement, not a substitute, to national-level sample surveys. Nor should it be seen as a turnkey solution. As shown in Part 3, indicators, data-collection methodology, analysis, and validation must be adapted to local conditions and developed over time. Enabling conditions also need to exist for CBMS to be effectively institutionalized. These include decentralization, public participation, political will, and adequate human and financial resources.

The challenges of institutionalizing CBMS also need to be recognized. These include the difficulties of integration within well-established systems of national agencies and local governments, the accuracy of data, the sustainability of CBMS at the community level and resource constraints, and the management of tensions between different interest groups competing for limited public resources.

Lessons learned about the enabling conditions

Decentralization facilitates the adoption of CBMS

Local government autonomy in delivering development programs is a common denominator in all countries where CBMS is most successfully used. CBMS is intended to be implemented by local governments in partnership with communities to provide detailed data on all households in those communities. Decentralized planning, budgeting, resource allocation, and program management are important elements for CBMS to take root and develop organically as part of local public sector program planning. Officials — both national and local in most countries where CBMS has been tested — have made it clear that the system is highly suited for decentralized government functions and devolved fiscal and political authority.

CBMS can strengthen the capacity of local governments to meet the challenge of improving the lives of their constituents. As has been demonstrated in a number of countries, CBMS allows local governments to use easy-to-understand and appropriate information and analysis to formulate policies and programs that are responsive to people's needs. This promotes poverty reduction and helps governments to realistically move forward to meeting the MDGs.

Political commitment is key to sustainability

To succeed, CBMS requires strong political commitment on the part of local government. To be sustainable, it also requires the commitment of higher levels of government, both to implement the system and to use the data generated.

The Philippines team found that a formal agreement (a Memorandum of Agreement) between government and partners, setting out objectives and outputs, scope of work, allocation of responsibilities, timetables, and resource requirements, was essential.

Commitment is expressed in other ways in other countries. In Cambodia, for instance, the Royal Government's *Statistics Law* calls for a statistics/planning officer to be placed in every commune to work with communities and officials in collecting information. Plans are now underway for the National Institute of Statistics to establish a CBMS bureau within the ministry to coordinate CBMS activities country-wide.

Local governments committed to evidenced-based planning and budgeting create an ongoing demand for the timely, relevant data that CBMS can provide. A vibrant civil society also helps to implement CBMS and increases the use of the data. Research shows that choosing the right kind of partners is critical: a strong corps of CBMS researchers and local government officials willing to work hand-in-hand with local communities not only ensures that the right indicators are developed to monitor poverty, but also builds local capacity and empowers communities.

Public participation is important

Involving communities and other stakeholders in discussions and decisions on local public sector investments has proven to be important. Through the process of data validation and analysis, communities have worked closely with public planners, officials, and policymakers in helping to prioritize investments for poverty reduction. As important, the knowledge gained through CBMS has empowered local communities and fostered participation in the public policy process. It has also improved systems for local accountability by facilitating greater transparency in public investments, and stimulated demand by local communities for better governance and accountability.

CBMS is cost-effective

Like all initiatives that involve primary data collection, CBMS entails costs in collecting and processing data. And because it is a census instrument, scaling-up province- or nation-wide poses financial challenges for governments. But as Carmelita Ericta, administrator of the Philippine National Statistics Office, points out, governments should recognize that "Information gathering is not a cost but an investment. It has high payoffs in terms of better allocation of resources, better designed programs, and improved targeting of beneficiaries."

Financing for CBMS should come largely from those who will benefit from the data generated, not external donors. IDRC's contribution has been designed to support the pilots of CBMS initiatives, in partnership with others, and has been directed to providing the technical guidance and capacity building needed for sustainability. Since local governments are the primary users of data, they should provide the bulk of the resources for implementing the system. In the Philippines, the provincial, municipal/city, and *barangay* governments provide the funds to implement CBMS in their localities.

CBMS can also generate savings and attract additional funding. Local governments have learned that the system helps to make best use of scarce public resources by better targeting programs and reducing discretionary spending. For example, the municipality of Sta. Elena of Camarines Norte in the Philippines was planning to allocate 220 000 pesos (US$4 500) for a feeding program to address child malnutrition. The CBMS survey showed, however, that there were only 97 malnourished children. As a result, they needed to allocate less than 20% of the proposed budget to address this problem. This saving was possible only because those who really needed entitlements were identified through the survey.

In Vietnam, local governments and communities have recognized the value of information that CBMS provides and have invested scarce local finances and human resources into its implementation. In Ha Tay province, for example, officials pointed out that many people from the communes willingly volunteer their time to collect data, which they see as socially important.

On the web

THE LESSONS

While local financing is critical for CBMS sustainability, the survey results can attract additional funding from international donors to finance complementary, larger projects to meet identified needs. Donors tend to favour proposals when they can see that the projects respond directly to an actual problem and they can see who will benefit. This has certainly been the case in Cambodia.

Lessons learned about CBMS design and implementation

Partnerships between researchers, government officials, and communities are essential

The research team should include members with varied experience and expertise. As Bangladesh and the Philippines have shown, researchers need to be knowledgeable about information systems and have a keen interest in, understanding of, and patience for working with communities. Also important, the team should be familiar with the policy environment and understand the workings of administrative institutions and the local political establishment. Experience has shown that where there is a purely academic orientation, the application of data for public action is greatly constrained and the chances of institutionalizing the system are severely reduced.

To ensure that the CBMS can survive changes in local and national governments, the CBMS needs a stable partner at all levels. Notes Vietnam's Vu Tuan Anh: "To institutionalize the CBMS, there should be a close partnership between researchers and governmental authorities who are in charge of poverty reduction, and non-governmental organizations in local areas."

Enlisting and orienting the community determines success from the outset

As a report by the Senegal team notes: "The value of an information system is a given.... Rather it is more useful to reflect on whether or not the local community is ready to accommodate the monitoring system" (Sylla 2004).

The communities and other stakeholders should participate in CBMS planning from the outset. In all countries where CBMS has been tested, a series of meetings and workshops with local officials, NGOs, and civil society ensured that they understood the project, enlisted their support, and identified data needs. This local advocacy can take various forms. In Bangladesh, for instance, the team first carried out a thorough participatory rural appraisal to better understand the communities and to develop relationships with the villagers. The research team noted that this exercise considerably changed the attitudes of local government officials. Discussions also made residents more aware of their problems and the role service providers play in their locality. They were asked to report inefficient providers. "That way," says the report, "the feedback mechanism gives the poor a voice."

In Burkina Faso, the pilot test convinced the research team to carry out an awareness-raising activity before conducting the survey. The researchers also found that the collection methodology needed to be clearly explained to all involved to avoid misunderstandings.

Selecting indicators and developing survey tools require research

The utility and success of any CBMS hinge on the selection of indicators. Developing this set requires first analyzing and comparing poverty-monitoring systems in use, determining how poverty can be defined in the community, and developing those indicators.

Trials in all countries have shown that a set of core indicators on the multi-dimensional aspects of poverty is needed. These indicators need to be simple enough for the enumerators to collect and community members to understand. In fact, field tests in a number of countries, such as Burkina Faso, led to a review and simplification of the indicators originally selected where it was found that lengthy questionnaires reduced the quality of responses.

Using the core set of indicators in all localities allows for aggregation at higher levels, thus increasing the usefulness of the data. Adding locally specific indicators increases utility at the community and local government levels. In Senegal, Vietnam, and the Philippines, for instance, the CBMS researchers found that different indicators needed to be introduced for different geographic regions.

The indicators also need to be revised periodically and evolve as local conditions change. Indicators related to emerging concerns may need to be incorporated in the system. Moreover, further use and analysis of the data to come up with new composite indices or targeting mechanisms may be necessary to respond to the needs of decision-makers. All these require ongoing research.

The design of survey tools — questionnaires — must take into account the knowledge levels of the local population, as well as the availability of data-processing equipment and software. Everywhere, recruiting local enumerators was found to increase community buy-in, build capacity, and increase the prospects for sustainability. But, as in Burkina Faso, this often requires reviewing and amending the questionnaire, rendering it into a user-friendly medium, and translating it into local languages.

Adequate training should not be underestimated
Training is critical to successfully implementing a CBMS. This is particularly so in communities with low literacy skills. In almost all countries where CBMS has been introduced, the teams initially underestimated the time needed for training, particularly for data processing and analysis.

Computerized data processing helps to speed up analysis, and an electronic database is easier and quicker to consult. But it is a viable option only where local human, technical, and financial resources exist.

Data collection and processing must be done in a timely manner

Time is of the essence in carrying out the survey, in processing, and in feeding results back to the community.

In the Philippines, it was determined that surveys should start soon after the training. The team has found that a month is usually sufficient time for the survey to be completed. Experience there shows that an enumerator can interview, on average, 10 households a day. And, of course, enumerators must be literate.

In a number of countries, it was found that qualitative and quantitative methods of data collection should be used in tandem. This was particularly obvious in Vietnam and Bangladesh. Teams in these countries supplemented the questionnaire with group discussions and interviews with key community informants.

Accurate processing is critical. Whether this is done manually or by computer — or a mixture of both — depends on the capacity and resources of the local government implementing CBMS.

Computerized processing has evolved through the years and from on-the-ground experiences. In the Philippines, local government partners experienced difficulties in using Microsoft Excel and the initial encoding sheets developed by the CBMS team. A more efficient, user-friendly encoding system — based on the Census and Survey Processing (CSPro System) — was therefore adopted. This freeware from the US Bureau of Census is designed to process household censuses and surveys. The solution to processing problems is the CBMS Indicator Simulator, developed by the team and made available free of charge.

On the web
THE LESSONS

In Cambodia, the lack of electricity did not deter the CBMS research team from exploring ways to use computers in processing the data — they used a car battery to power a laptop computer and a printer. This technology can be promoted in other CBMS areas with limited or no access to electricity.

Validating the data is essential

Community validation not only allows the CBMS team to test the reliability of data, but it also builds understanding within the communities of the dimensions of poverty and development. In so doing, it helps to empower communities, increase local ownership, and to mobilize communities for development programs.

In Senegal, for example, it was found that enumerators and their supervisors were best placed to lead the validation process. Experiences described in Part 3 of this book demonstrate the importance of bringing together government, civil society, and the community to validate results. Not only does this ensure that all the community learns about survey results, but it also provides an avenue to verify the accuracy of the findings and to provide explanations for unexpected outcomes.

The validation meeting also serves as a venue for identifying major problems and possible interventions, and facilitating the integration of CBMS results in the community's development and investment plans and socio-economic profile.

Dissemination is crucial

Returning the data to all stakeholders is central to CBMS. Meetings, workshops, community scorecards and Village Books, CD-ROMs, and newsletters — even traveling caravans — have all been used to present the results to communities, enabling them to set priorities and seek solutions to problems. In Bangladesh, for example, a village information book was prepared and planning workshops organized for service-delivery agencies, local government representatives, and villagers. The data book enabled the local government to identify needy households and record actions taken, thus helping to avoid duplication. The data also allowed local government to say no to demands not based on evidence.

Validation and dissemination go hand in hand in empowering the community. The process provides them with information and a process through which they can actively participate in planning. It enables them to develop a keen sense of their priorities and — on the basis of evidence — to articulate their needs to city planning officers. Armed with hard information on their condition, they are able to have more of a say in the allocation of public resources. And they can demand accountability and transparency on the part of government officials.

Obviously, CBMS can raise expectations that are difficult to meet. This points to the need for CBMS to provide communities and local governments with realistic information about local conditions, and to develop strategies for linking research to policy and practice. It also underlines the need for patience.

CBMS is a two-way process

These experiences have also yielded another lesson: the capacity of local governments to draw upon knowledge within communities, and for communities to learn about local government processes and governance. The CBMS process is not just about the flow of community and household information to local government planners, but also of information about policies and programs to communities, about government capacities and limitations, and about accountability. Communication often involves innovations to make this process better understood, and to take CBMS further than originally conceived. Burkina Faso's rendering of CBMS data in the form of pictures is one such innovation.

Among other innovations, the Philippine CBMS team prepares poverty maps from spot maps — drawings of the location of households and major infrastructure facilities in the community. These maps show relative locations of households and service facilities and are adequate to meet the objectives of CBMS. Some of the more advanced local governments have started to use global positioning systems to determine the location of their major infrastructure facilities and then situate housing units. Geo-referencing some of the major landmarks in the community can be useful, particularly for rescue operations following natural disasters.

Lessons learned about the benefits of CBMS

The experimentation with and implementation of CBMS around the world has also yielded information about the benefits of the system, some obvious, others less so.

Throughout this volume, it has been shown that CBMS

➤ empowers the community by building its capacity to participate in diagnosing the problem, offering solutions, and monitoring the impact of these solutions;

➤ enriches local government databases as well as those at higher levels;

➤ enhances the preparation of socio-economic profiles, as well as development and investment plans;

➤ improves the allocation of resources by making it easier to prioritize interventions based on the local poverty diagnosis;

➤ increases equity in resource allocation between communities and households, as well as between men and women; and

➤ helps to monitor the impact of projects and programs, thus contributing to poverty-reduction efforts.

CBMS pilots have also created strong research-to-policy links. Policymakers — especially those at the local level — have adopted CBMS as a powerful tool to inform policy decisions. Not only has micro data provided the contextual basis that helps local authorities respond effectively to development needs, but policy-makers themselves have often said that the system makes good political sense.

CBMS also increases transparency and accountability of local governments in resource allocation, thereby improving governance. In this way, it is a support mechanism for implementing decentralization policies being pursued around the world. And as this book has shown, CBMS data yields real benefits for communities, including new facilities such as schools, roads, and markets. It has also helped mobilize communities to address some of their own problems.

Extending CBMS uses and benefits

While this book has focused on the implementation of CBMS to monitor poverty at the local level, benefits also accrue at higher geopolitical levels. At a national level, for instance, CBMS data can help validate poverty analyses by offering a disaggregated look at household or community poverty profiles. It can also trace the evolution of poverty over time in a given community and at household levels, thereby providing insights into the dynamics of poverty transitions. This can help design safety nets and redistributive mechanisms and inform policies to better target programs and interventions.

The monitoring systems are being used in a number of other ways, to meet different needs. For instance, UNDP is exploring CBMS as an alternative to weak national information systems in West Africa to better understand energy use and energy poverty at community and household levels, and to monitor access to services. CBMS is being tested in the Philippines to facilitate local-level gender-responsive budgeting. And in both Cambodia and Vietnam, the systems are being used to target households for social protection programs, such as health entitlements and cash transfers.

The data is also proving useful to the private sector. In December 2007, for instance, Fenway International, Inc. — a Canadian cement producer investing in Palawan province in the Philippines — used CBMS results for the municipalities of Sofronio Española, Quezon, and Narra to identify areas for its various social development projects, including schools, *barangay* clinics, and farm-to-market roads.

Some of the ways in which CBMS is evolving and the challenges this poses are explored in Part 5.

Ways Forward

CBMS was designed principally as an instrument to monitor poverty at the local level. However, the system also lends itself to other uses, such as assessing the impacts of specific public investment and donor programs, tracking progress toward achieving the MDGs at local levels, and building up databases on vulnerability for use in early warning systems. The use of CBMS is also now being mainstreamed in gender-responsive budgeting in some regions, helping governments and planners allocate resources more equitably.

Monitoring public expenditures and donor programs

As demonstrated in this book, CBMS is more than simply a poverty-monitoring exercise. It is a process through which communities can actively participate in public policy to identify appropriate interventions, plan investments, and hold public officials to account: it is thus an instrument of good governance at the local level.

On the web
THE LESSONS

Communities and civil society partners involved with local governments in implementing CBMS around the world have attested to being empowered through the knowledge gained of their communities and the opportunity provided to work with researchers and local government planners in deciding what interventions will best improve well-being. This kind of social contract between communities and local governments has also led to an active interest in public budgets and development plans. Local governments have found it useful to demonstrate the efficiency and effectiveness of spending in a more transparent fashion. They have also used CBMS to obtain resources from central governments and donor agencies.

In Cambodia, for example, the National Institute of Statistics, in partnership with the governor, local government department heads, and commune councillors in Kratie province, have used CBMS to effectively plan targeted development programs and to regularly monitor expenditures. They also see the system as an expression of good local governance, and recognize that this will help attract resources from external donors. Similarly in other Asian countries, CBMS has demonstrated its usefulness as a policy instrument at the local level for budgetary oversight and resource mobilization.

With the regular conduct of censuses, CBMS can help identify a menu of cost-effective poverty-reduction initiatives to meet different needs. The impact of poverty-reduction programs and projects can be regularly monitored and assessed. This can also lead to further support of effective programs and the termination of ineffective ones.

Piloting CBMS for gender-responsive budgeting

CBMS aims to facilitate the rational allocation of resources. This is achieved by ensuring that the necessary information is available for evidence-based planning and budgeting. A more specific recent initiative is the use of CBMS to facilitate "gender-responsive" budgeting (Budlender et al. 2006).

Gender-responsive budgeting initiatives primarily aim to ensure the equitable allocation of government budgets. The goals are

➤ to reflect the different needs and priorities of men and women, girls and boys, in policies and budgets;

➤ to signal that these should not be assumed to be identical; and

➤ to ensure that the services and other elements funded through budgets cater to different needs and priorities.

Gender-responsive budgeting is not about having a separate budget for women, allotting a specific amount of money to women-specific programs, nor is it about dividing the budget equally. Rather, it is a mechanism for mainstreaming gender into the entire budget process, from analyzing the gendered situation that needs to be addressed to formulating plans and budgets that take into account gender- specific needs, to monitoring and evaluating whether funded activities have helped to rectify gender imbalances.

A pilot project to facilitate gender-responsive budgeting through CBMS was carried out in Escalante City in the Philippines in 2006. As Godofredo Reteracion, Escalante's city planning and development coordinator, explains, disaggregating the data by gender revealed that child mortality and malnutrition rates were higher for girls than for boys, and that women were under-represented in the labour force and in community and political life. Boys, on the other hand, had higher rates of non-attendance at school. The CBMS process was enhanced by focus group discussions to gather information that could not be collected from structured questionnaires. A computerized template was then developed to facilitate planning and budgeting to respond to the problems identified through the CBMS. This template allows the impact of the programs to be monitored by gender.

On the web
THE LESSONS

For gender-responsive budgeting, CBMS fills the data vacuum that hampers both pre- and post-budget analysis. It also provides a platform to regularly monitor the impacts of budgets in terms of their gender responsiveness.

The pilot in the Philippines has shown that it is indeed possible to formulate gender-responsive plans and budgets using the "engendered" CBMS. In Escalante, for example, the rather indiscriminate use of the gender and development budget was stopped and the funds were redirected to programs that responded to CBMS findings — a supplemental school feeding program, for example, women's health and safe motherhood programs, maternal and child care, and free hospitalization at local government hospitals, among other measures, were included in the city's 2008 gender and development plan and budget.

Tracking progress toward the MDGs

The need to track progress toward achieving the MDGs at sub-national levels has increased the demand for CBMS. And as has been shown, there is a significant correspondence between MDG and CBMS indicators.

Greater advocacy is needed, however, to inform other countries about the usefulness of CBMS in tracking MDG progress at the local level. There is a general assumption that monitoring the goals is a task for national statistical agencies mandated to report aggregates to national MDG coordinators. But the real value of tracking progress lies at the local level, where regional disparities and differences can reveal different circumstances and socio-economic factors, which can be isolated and analyzed by CBMS.

Building capacity is necessary for countries to be able to do this. The CBMS Network has an important role to play in sharing knowledge about how this can be accomplished.

Better targeting of program beneficiaries

By providing relevant information at household and individual levels, CBMS can provide details about the poor, not just by province or district, but by municipality and lower administrative levels. More importantly, because CBMS is a census and not a sample survey, it puts names and faces to the poor. And with the use of CBMS poverty maps, it is also possible to provide their address.

Why target? Because there are limited public resources and it is crucial that these benefit the neediest. The application of CBMS for targeting subsidies such as cash transfers, health entitlements, or credit can ensure that the intended transfers reach the poor and that there are overall cost savings.

How do we identify the poor using CBMS data? Composite indicators can be obtained from the CBMS core indicators to reflect the multi-dimensional nature of poverty. The CBMS composite index combines the 14 core indicators, indicating the number of unmet needs relating to health, nutrition, education, income, employment, housing, access to water and sanitation facilities, and peace and order in a household. A CBMS composite index of 4 indicates that 4 out of the 14 household needs represented by the core indicators are not met. Alternatively, a "proxy means" test model can also be obtained from CBMS data: by using data on assets owned, socio-economic characteristics, demographic characteristics, and spatial attributes, a measure of income or poverty status can be estimated. The estimated income or poverty status can then be used to determine eligibility to a program.

In short, CBMS can facilitate targeting by providing information on eligible beneficiaries for specific programs. Sector-specific indicators can also be used to identify who should receive the intervention.

On the web
THE LESSONS

Sounding an early warning

CBMS can provide an early warning of impending social crisis. Indicators can show how households and individuals are being affected by natural or manufactured shocks, and governments can then implement appropriate interventions to mitigate the impacts of these shocks.

In 1998, for example, Filippinos were living through a severe El Niño and an Asia-wide financial crisis. A CBMS survey in the Philippines at this time showed increased malnutrition among young children and an increased drop-out rate of school-age children. With this data, governments were able to design targeted interventions.

The current global financial crisis is the most recent example of a manufactured shock. CBMS can provide sentinel sites, or "poverty observatories," that can monitor the impact of the financial crisis on poverty. Indicators of unemployment, school participation, and malnutrition, for example, will be useful in monitoring short-term impact and in designing interventions.

Extending the reach of CBMS

Extending the use of CBMS for these and other purposes requires commitment by all levels of government. It also requires establishing formal links between national and local poverty monitoring systems. National systems can build the capacity of local government units to collect, process, and analyze data, and they can provide the statistical standards to ensure the comparability of CBMS and national survey data.

The simplicity and ease by which CBMS can be standardized at the local level also has enormous potential for integration into national poverty monitoring systems. For example, the 2004 PRSP for Burkina Faso adopts this approach by setting out only

10 core indicators to monitor human poverty, which corresponds to the CBMS.

CBMS has been expanding throughout Asia and Africa, and is now taking root in Latin America, demonstrating its versatility as a poverty-monitoring tool. But, as has been shown, CBMS is not a fixed system that is transported from one country to the next. While some basic features are necessary regardless of location, the list of indicators should be adapted to the local context. And differences in government structures across countries can also imply different focal institutions.

To date, CBMS has been piloted in 15 countries. Within these countries, greater advocacy is needed to institutionalize the system and make it part of local governments' regular activities, with national governments exercising an oversight function.

Sharing CBMS with other countries is now imperative. Partnerships with international organizations are key to spreading the message of CBMS' many uses. For instance, an experts group meeting on CBMS was organized by UNESCAP in 2006. The results of this meeting, presented during UNESCAP's 2006 Committee on Poverty Reduction meeting, have raised other countries' awareness of CBMS and has stimulated demand for its application. Similar initiatives would help put CBMS on other governments' agendas.

New avenues for research

While local poverty-monitoring systems have been developed in various countries in Asia and Africa, indicators that can measure different dimensions of poverty in other regions need to be developed and tested, and applied to show the faces of poverty in different contexts. There is also a need for further research to develop what can be termed as non-conventional indicators to capture dimensions of poverty that are not ordinarily measured and monitored, such as empowerment or human security.

On the web
THE LESSONS

Further research is also needed to enhance the use of CBMS for evidence-based policy-making and program implementation. One of the major uses of CBMS data is to identify the poor so that poverty-reduction programs can be directed to them. While this is already being done in several countries by using simple indicators, further research needs to be undertaken to come up with additional methodologies that use different indicators for identifying the poor.

Research is also needed to identify which poverty reduction programs truly are effective. The short-term and long-term impact of existing programs can be evaluated using CBMS data, particularly when CBMS has been installed for several years. This research could point to the need to further modify the CBMS design to include additional indicators to facilitate monitoring and evaluation functions.

Finally, as the gender-responsive budgeting project in the Philippines has shown, CBMS has proven itself to be an important if not fundamental instrument in guiding local governments in budget planning and evaluation. Further research is needed, however, to show how CBMS can be applied more vigorously on the expenditure side. Additional research on how CBMS data can be fed more systematically into planning and budgeting processes would also ensure more evidence-based decision-making. There is growing interest, for example, in linking CBMS more deeply to performance-based management of public budgets — at the local level, in different contexts, and particularly under different degrees of decentralization.

Interest in CBMS is also growing in countries that are attempting to implement participatory budgeting systems. The convergence between CBMS as a participatory monitoring system for public expenditure at the local level, and performance-based budgeting systems in local governments presents common ground for new explorations in governance and budgetary systems.

Glossary of Terms and Abbreviations

barangay – a village, the lowest political unit, Philippines

BBS – Bangladesh Bureau of Statistics

CBMS – Community-Based Monitoring System

CECI – Centre d'étude et de coopération internationale, Canada

CEDRES – Centre d'Étude, de Documentation et de Recherche Économique et Sociale, University of Ouagadougou, Burkina Faso

CIDA – Canadian International Development Agency

Comprehensive Development Framework – a set of principles promulgated by the World Bank to guide development and poverty reduction, including the provision of external assistance. The approach emphasizes the interdependence of all elements of development: social, structural, human, governance, environmental, economic, and financial.

commune – communal administrative unit or village, the lowest administrative unit, Vietnam

CREA – Centre de recherches économiques appliquées, Senegal

CSPro System – Census and Survey Processing System

decentralization – the process of bringing decision-making and governance closer to the people or citizens. It can include **political decentralization**, giving citizens or their elected representatives more power in public decision-making; **administrative decentralization**, redistributing authority, responsibility, and financial resources for providing public services among different levels of governance; and **fiscal decentralization**, enabling local governments to raise revenues and giving them the authority to make decisions about expenditures.

deconcentration – In Cambodia, deconcentration refers to the codification of an expanded role for provincial and district levels of government. It involves delegating activities from the central level and establishing funding mechanisms to support this delegation. Decentralization in Cambodia refers to the creation, regulation, and support of elected commune governments (Manor 1999).

DOLISA – Provincial Department of Labour, Invalids and Social Affairs, Vietnam

EMICoV – Enquête Modulaire Integrée sur les Conditions de Vie (integrated modular survey of household living conditions), Benin

Gender-responsive budgeting initiatives primarily aim to ensure the equitable allocation of government budgets. The goal is to reflect the different needs and priorities of men and women, girls and boys, in policies and budgets; to signal that these should not be assumed to be identical; and to ensure that the services and other elements funded through budgets cater to different needs and priorities.

GIS – geographic information system

HEPR – Program on Hunger Eradication and Poverty Reduction, Vietnman

HLSS – Household Living Standards Survey, Vietnam

INSD – Institut National de la Statistique et de la Démographie, Burkina Faso

kecamatan – a subdivision of a regency or city (both one administrative level lower than a province), Indonesia

kelurahan – a village, the lowest level of government administration, Indonesia

LGU – Local Government Unit. Under decentralization in the Philippines, LGUs are defined as the lowest level of government with assigned jurisdictional authority and with local autonomy as set out in the local government code of the Philippines (see www.dilg.gov.ph/LocalGovernmentCode.aspx#b1t1c1).

LLPMS – Local-Level Poverty-Monitoring System, Bangladesh

MDGs – United Nations Millennium Development Goals. A set of eight goals — which range from halving extreme poverty to halting the spread of HIV/AIDS and providing universal primary education by the target date of 2015 — agreed to by all the world's countries and all the world's leading development institutions in September 2000.

MIMAP – Micro Impacts of Macroeconomic and Adjustment Policies, a former IDRC program

MOLISA – Ministry of Labour, Invalids and Social Affairs, Vietnam

NAPC – National Anti-Poverty Commission, Philippines

NGO – non-governmental organization

NIS – National Institute of Statistics, Cambodia

NRDB – Natural Resource Database

NSC – National Statistics Centre, Lao PDR

OECD – Organisation for Economic Co-operation and Development

participatory rural appraisal – an approach used by NGOs and other international development agencies to incorporate the knowledge and opinions of rural people in planning and managing projects and programs

PME – **Participatory monitoring and evaluation** is a process through which stakeholders at various levels engage in monitoring or evaluating a particular project, program, or policy, share control over the content, the process, and the results of the activity, and engage in taking or identifying corrective actions.

poverty line – the minimum level of income deemed necessary to achieve an adequate standard of living in a given country. The World Bank defines extreme economic poverty as living on less than US$1.25 per day (at 2005 prices, adjusted to account for the most recent differences in purchasing power across countries).

PPDO – Provincial Planning and Development Office, Philippines

PRSP – Poverty Reduction Strategy Paper. This document is required by the International Monetary Fund and World Bank before a country can be considered for debt relief within the Heavily Indebted Poor Countries initiative. It describes a country's macroeconomic, structural, and social policies and programs to promote growth and reduce poverty, as well as associated external financing needs.

SEILA program – an aid-mobilization and coordination framework to support Cambodia's decentralization and deconcentration reforms, launched in 1999 and completed in 2006

structural adjustment programs – economic policies that countries must follow to qualify for new World Bank and International Monetary Fund loans and help them make debt repayments on older debts owed to commercial banks, governments, and the World Bank. They have common guiding principles and features, including export-led growth, privatization and liberalization, and the efficiency of the free market.

subsidiarity – the principle that matters should be handled by the smallest or lowest competent authority

Union Parishad – the third tier of local government in Bangladesh comprised of a collection of village-level (*gram parishads*) units

Upazila – a sub-district: Bangladesh's intermediate local government level, introduced with decentralization in the mid-1980s

UNDP – United Nations Development Programme

UNESCAP – United Nations Economic and Social Commission for Asia and the Pacific

VDGs – Vietnam Development Goals

WDR – *World Development Report*, published annually by the World Bank

Sources and Resources

All background papers from past PEP Research Network General Meetings, and various other PEP and CBMS Network documents and working papers listed in this appendix, may be found on the PEP website (**www.pep-net.org**). Many other relevant documents and CBMS research reports are available from the archived IDRC MIMAP website (**www.idrc.ca/en/ev-6824- 201-1-DO_TOPIC. html**) and as part of the Globalization, Growth, and Poverty Community on the IDRC Digital Library (**idl-bnc.idrc.ca/dspace/ handle/123456789/13**).

Cited references

Asselin, L.M.; Vu T.A. 2005. *Multidimensional poverty monitoring: a methodology and implementation in Vietnam.* Paper presented at the 4th PEP Research Network General Meeting, 13–17 June 2005, Colombo, Sri Lanka.

Attanasso, M.O. 2007. *Report on the census of the living conditions of the households of the 13th District of Cotonou.* Paper presented to the 6th PEP Research Network General Meeting, June 14–16 June 2007, Lima, Peru.

Budlender, D.; Reyes, C.; Melesse, M. 2005. *Gender-responsive budgeting through the CBMS lens.* PIDS Discussion Paper 2006-17, Philippines Institute for Development Studies, Manila, Philippines. **ideas.repec.org/p/phd/dpaper/dp_2006-17.html**

CBMS (Community-Based Monitoring System Network). 2008. "Mayor of Cotonou, Benin, bares 6-point agenda in light of CBMS results," *CBMS Network Updates* Vol.V No. 2, March 2008. **www.pep-net.org/new-pep/Group/CBMS/Other% 20meets/ newsletter/CBMS%20Updates%20Issues/March 2008_final.pdf**

Chen, S.; Ravallion, M. 2008. "The developing world is poorer than we thought, but no less successful in the fight against poverty," *Policy Research Working Paper 4703*, World Bank, Washington, DC, USA. **go.worldbank.org/DPZY24X240**

Guha, R.K. 2006. *Planning for poverty reduction at the grassroots: experience of LLPMS.* Paper presented at the 5th PEP Research Network General Meeting, 18–22 June 2006, Addis Ababa, Ethiopia.

Hettige S. 2005. *Poverty monitoring, empowerment of local communities and decentralized planning in Sri Lanka.* PEP Working Paper 2005-05, PEP, Manila, Philippines.

_____ 2007. *Community-based poverty monitoring in Sri Lanka.* Paper presented to the 6th PEP Research Network General Meeting, 14–16 June 2007, Lima, Peru.

Jolly, R. 1991. "Adjustment with a human face: A UNICEF record and perspective on the 1980s," *World Development,* 19(12).

Jütting, J.; Kauffmann, C.; McDonnell, I.; Osterrieder, H.; Pinaud, N.; Wegner, L. 2004. *Decentralisation and poverty in developing countries: exploring the impact.* DAC Working Paper 236, OECD Development Centre, Paris, France. **www.oecd.org/dataoecd/40/19/33648213.pdf**

Keosiphandone, P. 2007. *The uses of community-based monitoring system (CBMS) in the planning and monitoring process in Saravan, Lao PDR.* Paper presented to the 6th PEP Research Network General Meeting, 14–16 June 2007, Lima, Peru.

Konate, I.; Somda, P.; Kone, M. 2007. *Analyse des résultats de l'enquête dans le département de Koper, février/mai 2007.*

Manor, J. 1999. *The political economy of democratic decentralization.* The World Bank, Washington, DC, USA.

Mujeri, M.K.; Guha, R.K, 2003. *Local Level Poverty Monitoring System in Bangladesh: some lessons from the pilot survey.* CBMS Working Paper 2003-1.

Reyes, C.; Ilarde, K.C. 1996. *A community-based monitoring system for poverty tracking.* MIMAP Research Paper No. 24, IDRC, Ottawa, ON, Canada. **www.idrc.ca/en/ev-64811-201-1-DO_TOPIC.html**

Saumier, M.A.; Habito, C.F.; Njinkeu, D.; 2004. *External review of the MIMAP Program Initiative: report submitted to the International Development Research Centre, March 2004.* IDRC, Ottawa, ON, Canada. **www.idrc.ca/en/ev-113886-201-1-DO_TOPIC.html**

Scott, C. 2005. *Measuring up to the measurement problem: the role of statistics in evidence-based policy-making.* PARIS21, Paris, France. **www.paris21.org/documents/2086.pdf**

Sen, A. 1999. *Development as freedom.* Oxford University Press, Oxford, UK.

Sothearith, T.; Net, K.; Nisaykosal, N. 2006. *Working towards a nationwide commune-based monitoring system for Cambodia.* Paper presented to the 5th PEP Research Network General Meeting, 18–22 June 2006, Addis Ababa, Ethiopia.

Suryadarma, D.; Akmadi, H.; Toyamah, N. 2005. *Objective measures of family welfare for individual targeting: results from pilot project on community-based monitoring system in Indonesia.* PEP Working Paper 2005-10, PEP, Manila, Philippines.

Sylla, M.B. 2004. CBMS–Sénégal: un dispositif de suivi des conditions de vie des ménages à l'échellon d'une collectivité locale (version provisoire). MIMAP report Senegal.

Vu, T.A. 2007. *Implementation of CBMS in Vietnam.* Paper presented to the 6th PEP Research Network General Meeting, 14–16 June 2007, Lima, Peru.

UN (United Nations). 2007. *The Millennium Development Goals Report 2007.* UN, New York, NY, USA. **mdgs.un.org/unsd/mdg/Resources/Static/Products/Progress2007/UNSD_MDG_Report_2007e.pdf**

_____ 2008. *The Millennium Development Goals Report 2008.* UN, New York, NY, USA. **mdgs.un.org/unsd/mdg/Resources/Static/Products/Progress2008/MDG_Report_2008_En.pdf**

UNDP (United Nations Development Programme). 2007. *Human Development Report 2007/2008.* UNDP, New York, NY, USA. **hdr.undp.org/en/reports/global/hdr2007-2008/**

World Bank. 1990. *World Development Report 1990: poverty.* World Bank, Washington DC, USA. **go.worldbank.org/S5W4W40A31**

_____ 2000. *World Development Report 2000/2001: attacking poverty*. World Bank, Washington, DC, USA. **go.worldbank.org/L8RGH3WLI0**

_____ 2005. *Decentralization in the Philippines: strengthening local government financing and resource management in the short term*. World Bank, Washington, DC, USA. **go.worldbank.org/A9UUBQ9IV0**

_____ 2006. Forum on National Plans as Poverty Reduction Strategies in East Asia, 4–6 April 2006, Vientiane, Lao PDR. World Bank, Washington, DC, USA. **go.worldbank.org/14OG84SM00**

Additional reading

Bautista, V.A. 2007. "Fighting poverty: lessons learned from community-based monitoring system implementation — highlights of case studies," *JOAAG*, 2(1). **joaag.com/uploads/Bautista.pdf**

Bautista, V.A.; Alfonso, O.M. 2006. *Learning from CBMS implementation: selected case studies*. Angelo King Institute, De LaSalle University, Manila, Philippines.

Bidya, S. 2007. *Replication of CBMS in Dodoma Municipality: towards scaling up and institutionalization of the system in Tanzania*. Paper presented to the 6th PEP Research Network General Meeting, 14–16 June 2007, Lima, Peru.

Budlender, D; Reyes, C:, Melesse M. 2008. *Facilitating evidence-based and gender-responsive budgeting through the use of CBMS: lessons from pilot projects*. Community-based Monitoring System (CBMS) Network. **www.idrc.ca/en/ev-129784-201-1-DO_TOPIC.html**

CBMS Network Coordinating Team. 2002–2005. *CBMS Working Papers*. **www.pep-net.org/NEW-PEP/HTML/PEPWorkingPapers. html#CBMS**

_____ 2003–2008. *CBMS Network Updates.* **www.pep-net.org/ new-pep/Group/CBMS/cbms_newsletter.htm**

_____ 2004. *Institutionalizing the CBMS approach to poverty monitoring in selected countries.* Proceedings of the 2003 CBMS Network Meeting, 4–8 November 2003, Hanoi, Vietnam.

_____ 2004. *The evolving role of CBMS amidst changing environments.* Proceedings of the 2004 CBMS Network Meeting, 16–24 June 2004, Senegal and Burkina Faso.

_____ 2005. *Gaining insights on the CBMS application: the case of the Philippines.* Proceeding of the 2004 National Conference on CBMS, 23–24 September 2004, Makati City, Philippines.

_____ 2006. *New challenges for the CBMS: seeking opportunities for a more responsive role.* Proceedings of the 2005 CBMS Network Meeting, 13–17 June 2005, Colombo, Sri Lanka.

_____ 2007. *CBMS: looking beyond poverty monitoring.* Proceedings of the 2006 CBMS Network Meeting, 18–22 June 2006, Addis Ababa, Ethiopia.

Chambers, R. 1997. *Whose reality counts? Putting the first last,* Intermediate Technology Publications Ltd, London, UK. **developmentbookshop.com/product_info.php?products_id=358**

Coronel, J.M. 2007. *Development of a community-based monitoring system in the Northern Region of Peru.* Paper presented to the 6th PEP Research Network General Meeting, 14–16 June 2007, Lima, Peru.

Keolangsy, S. 2007. *Community-based poverty monitoring system in Lao PDR.* Paper presented to the 6th PEP Research Network General Meeting, 14–16 June 2007, Lima, Peru.

Konate, I.; Somda, P.; Kone, M. 2004. *Poverty monitoring system in Burkina Faso: the case of Yako Division in the Passore Province.* Research report, June/July 2003.

Lamberte, M.B.; Orbeta, A.C.; Lapar, M.L.A. 1991. *Micro Impacts of Macroeconomic Adjustment Policies (MIMAP): a framework paper and review of literature.* PIDS Working Paper 1991-02. Philippine Institute for Development Studies, Manila, Philippines. **ideas.repec.org/p/phd/wpaper/wp_1991-02.html**

Mandap, A.B. 2001. *Utilizing a community-based monitoring system for development planning in the Province of Palawan.* MIMAP Research Paper No. 52. IDRC, Ottawa, ON, Canada. **www.idrc.ca/en/ev-64903-201-1-DO_TOPIC.html**

Muro, R.K. 2007. *Implementation of community-based poverty monitoring system in Tanzania.* Paper presented to the 6th PEP Research Network General Meeting, 14–16 June 2007, Lima, Peru.

Narayan-Parker, D. 1997. *Voices of the poor: poverty and social capital in Tanzania.* World Bank, Washington, DC, USA. **go.worldbank.org/DWDXIW5WG0**

Natural Resources Database: **www.nrdb.co.uk**

Panadero, A. 2005. *Localizing the Millennium Development Goals: CBMS as a tool for MDG benchmarking and poverty diagnosis and planning.* Paper presented at the 3rd National Conference on CBMS, 28-30 September 2005, Manila, Philippines.

PEP-CBMS Network Coordinating Team. 2007. *CBMS Network database/repository*. Paper presented to the 6th PEP Research Network General Meeting, 14–16 June 2007, Lima, Peru.

Phoueng, K. 2007. *Need and usage of commune data system in Kratie Province, Cambodia*. Paper presented to the 6th PEP Research Network General Meeting, 14–16 June 2007, Lima, Peru.

Reyes, M.T.; Abejo, S. 2006. *Mechanisms and initiatives for monitoring Philippines' progress in MDGs*. Paper presented to the UNESCAP/SIAP/UNDP/ADB Workshop on Statistics for Monitoring Achievement of the MDGs in Asia and the Pacific, 31 July – 2 August 2006, Bangkok, Thailand.

Reyes, C.; Alba, I.Z. 1994. *Assessement of community-based systems monitoring household welfare*. MIMAP Research Paper No. 15. IDRC, Ottawa, ON, Canada. **www.idrc.ca/en/ev-64753-201-1-DO_TOPIC.html**

Reyes, C.; Mandap, A.B.; Ilarde, K.; Garnace, L.; Asirot, J.; Bancoita, J. 2006. *Community-based monitoring system: a tool to fight poverty*. Unpublished paper.

Reyes, C.; Valencia, L.E. 2003. *Poverty reduction, decentralization and community-based monitoring systems*. Paper presented at the ADB–IDRC Seminar on Poverty, Trade, and Growth: Issues in Sustainable Development, 29–30 October 2003, Manila, Philippines.

Riggirozzi, M.P. 2003. *Bridging policy and poverty: Micro Impact of Macroeconomic and Adjustment Policies Program in Bangladesh*. IDRC, Ottawa, ON, Canada. **www.idrc.ca/en/ev-57584-201-1-DO_TOPIC.html**

Riggirozzi, M.P.; Tuplin, T. 2004. *The influence of research on policy: MIMAP-Philippines*. IDRC, Ottawa, ON, Canada. **www.idrc.ca/en/ev-57585-201-1-DO_TOPIC.html**

Soliman, C. 2004. Making democracy work and people empowerment real through the CBMS. Keynote address delivered to the 2004 National Conference on CBMS, 23–24 September 2004, Makati City, Philippines.

_____ 2004. *Gaining insights on the CBMS application: the case of the Philippines*. Proceedings of the 2004 National Conference on CBMS, 23–24 September 2004, Makati City, Philippines. **idl-bnc.idrc.ca/dspace/handle/123456789/33620**

Sothearith, T. 2004. *SEILA Program and role of Commune Database Information System (CDIS), Cambodia*. Paper presented to the PEP Research Network Meeting, 16–20 June 2004, Dakar, Senegal.

Tagoe, C. 2007. *The use of CBMS approach in data collection in analyzing the MDGs at the district level: case study of the Dangme West District in Ghana*. Paper presented to the 6th PEP Research Network General Meeting, 14–16 June 2007, Lima, Peru.

Tuplin, T. 2003. *The influence of research on policy: the case of MIMAP-Senegal*. IDRC, Ottawa, ON, Canada. **www.idrc.ca/en/ev-57583-201-1-DO_TOPIC.html**

Vipongxay, V. 2006. *Community-based monitoring system in Lao PDR: the survey in Sepon (Savanakhet) and Toolan Districts (Saravan)*. Paper presented to the 5th PEP Research Network General Meeting, 18–22 June 2006, Addis Ababa, Ethiopia.

Vu, T.T. 2007. *Using CBMS for monitoring women's advancement*. Paper presented to the 6th PEP Research Network General Meeting, 14–16 June 2007, Lima, Peru.

World Bank. 1987–1992. World Bank living standards measurement surveys. World Bank, Washington, DC, USA. go.worldbank.org/IPLXWMCNJ0

The Publisher

The International Development Research Centre is a Crown corporation created by the Parliament of Canada in 1970 to help researchers and communities in the developing world find solutions to their social, economic, and environmental problems. Support is directed toward developing an indigenous research capacity to sustain policies and technologies developing countries need to build healthier, more equitable, and more prosperous societies.

IDRC Books publishes research results and scholarly studies on global and regional issues related to sustainable and equitable development. As a specialist in development literature, IDRC Books contributes to the body of knowledge on these issues to further the cause of global understanding and equity. The full catalogue is available at **www.idrc.ca/books**.